W9-DDR-198

STRANGERS AT YOUR DOOR

How to Respond to

* Jehovah's Witnesses

* The Mormons

* Televangelists

* Cults, and More. . . .

STRANGERS

AT
YOUR
DOOR

How to Respond to

* Jehovah's Witnesses

* The Mormons

* Televangelists

* Cults, and More....

Albert J. Nevins, M.M.

Our Sunday Visitor Publishing Division
Our Sunday Visitor, Inc.
Huntington, Indiana 46750

Brief New Testament selections in this work are taken from the *New American Bible With Revised New Testament*, © 1986 by the Confraternity of Christian Doctrine, Washington, D.C.; Old Testament selections are taken from the *New American Bible*, © 1969, 1970 by the CCD. All Rights Reserved. No part of the *New American Bible With Revised New Testament* may be reproduced in any form without permission in writing from the copyright owner. An excerpt from the Order of the Mass is taken from the English translation of the Roman Missal, © 1973 by the International Committee on English in the Liturgy, Washington, D.C. All Rights Reserved. The author is also grateful for brief excerpts from various titles mentioned in the bibliography at the end of this book.

Copyright © 1988
by Our Sunday Visitor Publishing Division
Our Sunday Visitor, Inc.
All Rights Reserved

With the exception of short excerpts for critical reviews, no part of this book may be reproduced in any manner whatsoever without permission in writing from the publisher. *Write:*

Our Sunday Visitor Publishing Division
Our Sunday Visitor, Inc.
200 Noll Plaza
Huntington, Indiana 46750

International Standard Book Number: 0-87973-496-5
Library of Congress Catalog Card Number: 88-61111

Cover Design by Rebecca J. O'Brien

PRINTED IN THE UNITED STATES OF AMERICA
496

Contents

1

Strangers At Your Door

THEY COME to your doorstep, usually in pairs but sometimes alone, neat, well-dressed, and polite. Each of them usually carries a briefcase or some books under one arm. They are sincere, earnest, friendly, well-meaning people. They have been carefully trained in their techniques so that their approach is smooth, simple, and polite.

"Good afternoon, Mrs. Jones," they might begin (they have obtained your name from your mailbox or a neighbor). "We are visiting some of the homes in the neighborhood and would like to share with you the good news of God's love for us in the midst of a very difficult world. Surely, you must be concerned with what is going on about us — crime, hunger, wars, plagues such as AIDS."

"Yes, but . . . "

"All of these things have been foretold in the Bible. Do you read the Bible?"

"Not as much as I should."

"We would like to leave you with a plan for Bible reading. The Bible has the answers to today's problems. Here is a copy of our magazine, *Awake!*, in which you will find an article on how the Book of Revelation tells about what is happening to the world today. We will leave it with you."

Such an introduction accomplishes a number of things. It

involves you in a conversation in which you find nothing objectionable. It introduces you to some concerned and caring people who hope that you will be sufficiently impressed to invite them in so that they can go into greater detail, catch your interest, and be invited back.

Danger and Opportunity

What you do not know is that they are there to undermine belief in your own Faith so that you will accept theirs. While they may be using familiar terms, the meaning they attach to the words can be quite opposed to your understanding. While they have been systematically trained in their beliefs and approaches, few of those whom they accost have had similar training in their own faiths. The proselytizers' appeal is mainly to the religiously uneducated and the undiscriminating. To successfully counter the strangers at your door, you must know what you believe and why. You must be ready to ask your visitors questions and put them on the defensive so that they will examine their own beliefs.

But it is not only the person ringing your doorbell with whom you must be concerned. It can be the friendly young man or woman you meet on a college campus or in some other places where people gather — places which have become prime recruiting grounds for some of the most outrageous cults. Many a young person has begun a journey down the road to one of these movements by accepting an invitation to a meal or concert or lecture on happiness. Finally, there are some people already in your home whose overtures are revealed by simply flicking on a television or radio switch. These are the televangelists, all of whom are trying to convert you to their own interpretations of the Bible, interpretations that can range all the way from the relatively orthodox to the heretically weird.

The purpose of this book is to show you what you must believe to be a Catholic Christian, to explain how the teachings of these modern sects differ from traditional beliefs, to demonstrate that many of these sects or cults are but counterfeits of true Christianity, and to give you the means to reach out to these well-meaning but mistaken adherents and try to win them to your own beliefs.

In short, the stranger who comes to you should be seen as an opportunity to fulfill the missionary vocation which was conferred on you in baptism. Christ's command to "go and teach" was meant for each of His followers. It is tragic that those who promote the ideas of mere men should be so zealous, while those who possess God's truth should remain idle.

2

Apologetics

A POLOGETICS seems to have become a lost art. Once it was taught in Catholic schools, but today one simply does not hear the word used. Apologetics is that branch of theology devoted to the defense of the origin, authority, and teachings of the Church. Elements of apologetics exist in fundamental theology, but apologetics as apologetics — that is, a positive and reasoned defense of the Faith — is seldom taught. Perhaps the main reason lies in a misunderstanding of the ecumenism expounded by Vatican Council II.

Ecumenism Today

The Council in its *Decree on Ecumenism* involved the whole Church, clergy and laity alike, in seeking the theological unity demanded by Christ (Jn 17:11). St. Paul insisted on this unity, saying that all are called to recognize "one Lord, one faith, one baptism; one God and Father of all. . ." (Eph 4:5-6). To foster this communion of believers, the Church recognized its responsibility to enter into dialogue with other Christian bodies, separated in faith, theology, social contacts, behavior, and too often in love. The Secretariat for Promoting Christian Unity was established at the Vatican, and to date substantial dialogue has taken place between the Catholic Church and Orthodox, Coptics, Anglicans, Lutheran World Federation, World Alliance of Reformed Churches, World Methodist Council, Disciples of Christ, Baptist World Alliance, Pentecostal groups, and some Evangelicals. Contacts have also been made by another secretariat with non-Christian groups such as Buddhists and Muslims. Already from these talks have come new understandings and areas of agreement.

What ecumenism sought to do was to remove those attitudes which created enmity and rivalry, to avoid the evaluation of those creeds that differed from the Catholic Church as something to be condemned as heresy and schism, something to be denied existence. Ecumenism seeks to show that Catholics and their separated brothers and sisters are united in more areas than those in which they differ, that they have a common task before God, and that the Catholic Church recognizes the good will and faith of other Christians. The Catholic Church also recognized that there was much that could be learned from others.

Ecumenism does not mean the abandonment of one's own beliefs. Writing in *Sacramentum Mundi* (Herder and Herder, New York), Heinrich Beck correctly stated the Church's position when he said: "The Catholic Church of course is conscious of itself, now as always, as the Church in which the one Church of Christ subsists, and in its own understanding of its own nature (as part of its faith in the whole of the revelation of God in Jesus Christ), it simply cannot concede the same character to other Churches."

While the goal of full Christian unity may never be reached, it would be intolerable not to continue to seek it, not to adopt common actions in those areas in which agreement can be found. Much can be done by Christians together, not only in the social field but even in theology and Scripture. There are examples of such common activity in new translations of the Scriptures and in the agreement among churches on modes of expression. Common elements in liturgy have also been recognized. However, ecumenism does not mean that one cannot defend beliefs that are under attack, and this defense can only be properly made by one who is skilled in apologetics.

A Positive Apologetics

Apologetics is not to be regarded as a purely defensive measure. It should indicate a readiness to share one's faith with another. In His teaching, Our Lord compared the Faith to a city on a mountain or a lamp put out on a stand for all to see. The Gospel of Jesus is a universal Gospel, and the mission to make it known has been entrusted to every Christian. Hence, we must be more than ready to share our beliefs; we must, in fact, take positive steps to make known His message. Vatican II saw the whole Church in mission, and the new Code of Canon Law reminds each Catholic that his or her basic vocation is a missionary one. Therefore, those who come to our door to share their beliefs are an opportunity for us to show them what we believe ourselves. Apologetics, then, is a response to our own faith, made not combatively but in a way that allows our own missionary vocation free rein. Faith, like love, cannot be forced. It must be won by truth and charity.

Apologetics has varied over the centuries in answering challenges to the Faith. The apologetics of the early Christian Church was a response to the paganism of Rome and a hedonistic Hellenic culture. The truths which Christianity presented were in sharp contrast to the spirit of the times, and this very polarization attracted controversy in itself. Later came the militant inroads of Islam, which often prompted a militant response. The Reformation unleashed a doctrinal attack on the Church, and the response was a defensive circling of the wagons and an apologetics of a Church under siege. The Enlightenment brought intellectual challenges to the Faith.

When the waves of European immigration swept over the United States in the nineteenth century, Catholic immigrants found themselves in great difficulties. Their Faith was misunderstood and held in suspicion.

Bishop James Gibbons (later a cardinal) recognized that the immigrants needed confirmation in their beliefs and a way to show the reasonableness of these beliefs to others. The result in 1876 was his apologetic work, *The Faith of Our Fathers*, a book that went through many editions and sold in the millions (currently reprinted by Tan Books, Rockford, Ill.). He told the story of the Catholic Faith in biblical terms and thus appealed to open-minded Protestants. The result was many conversions. In 1913, Father John Francis Noll (later an archbishop), a pastor in Huntington, Indiana, published his book, *Father Smith Instructs Jackson*, to combat ignorance of the Catholic Church and its teachings. This book answered questions non-Catholics raise about the Faith; it went through many editions and is still in print today (Our Sunday Visitor Publishing, Huntington, Ind.). Later, Father John A. O'Brien brought out his *The Faith of Millions*, the aim of which was not controversy but an exposition of the doctrinal and sacramental structure of the Church. This book is also still in print (OSV Publishing, Huntington, Ind.).

What these books demonstrated was that apologetics was a reasoned demonstration of the truths of the Catholic Faith, using creditable and acceptable historical, philosophical, and scriptural argument.

This present book does not aim to be a work of apologetics, but we have dwelt on this subject to emphasize its importance in the modern scheme of conversion of oneself and others. Apologetics must be a familiar science for the believer in order to confirm his or her own beliefs, and by doing so to be able to present those beliefs to others, not in a watered-down version to approximate the level of the unbeliever, but as an uncompromising presentation of the teachings of Jesus.

3

What Catholics Must Believe

ASK THE AVERAGE Catholic what he or she believes and the answer will be something like, "I believe in God; I believe in Jesus Christ and His Gospel; I believe in the Catholic Church," and let it go at that. Pushed, the Catholic will come up with more beliefs, but the answers will be disorganized and not comprehensive. Yet each Catholic recites his or her beliefs every Sunday at Mass, often without too much reflection on what is being said. This affirmation of belief is done in the recitation of the Creed after the Gospel and homily.

This systematic presentation of basic beliefs came about in the early Church in response to disputes over the meaning of Gospel passages, principally over the divinity of Jesus Christ. The Fathers of the Church met in the first general council at Nicea in 325. They wanted to defend Scripture against misinterpretation and to confirm the Apostolic Faith of the Church. They did this in the composition of a creed that is still recited and which unites the Churches of East and West. This creed states the basic beliefs necessary to be considered Catholic:

The Nicene Creed

We believe in one God,
  the Father, the Almighty,

15

maker of heaven and earth,
of all that is seen and unseen.

We believe in one Lord, Jesus Christ,
the only Son of God, eternally begotten of the Father,
God from God, Light from Light,
true God from true God,
begotten, not made, one in being with the Father.

Through him all things were made.
For us men and for our salvation
he came down from heaven:
by the power of the Holy Spirit
he was born of the Virgin Mary, and became man.

For our sake he was crucified under Pontius Pilate;
he suffered, died, and was buried.
On the third day he arose again
in fulfillment of the Scriptures;
he ascended into heaven
and is seated at the right hand of the Father.
He will come again in glory to judge the living and the dead,
and his kingdom will have no end.

We believe in the Holy Spirit, the Lord, the giver of life,
who proceeds from the Father and the Son.
With the Father and Son he is worshipped and glorified.
He has spoken through the prophets.

We believe in one, holy, catholic and apostolic Church.
We acknowledge one baptism for the forgiveness of sins.
We look for the resurrection of the dead,
and the life of the world to come. Amen.

This is the basic statement of faith for every Catholic and it is one to which other Christians also give assent. This creed commits us to these important beliefs:

1. A trinitarian God of one nature but three personalities: Father, Son and Holy Spirit.
2. Jesus Christ, eternally God, but made man through the power of the Holy Spirit and the cooperation of the Virgin Mary.
3. Our redemption and salvation through Jesus Christ, who will also be our judge.
4. The Holy Spirit, the animator, eternally God, proceeding from the Father and Son and enlightening the Church.
5. God's Church that is one, holy, catholic and apostolic.
6. Baptism, forgiving sins, resurrection, eternal life.

Over the centuries, this Creed has been explained in its implications and details, producing other dogmas derived from it. These have resulted in our catechisms, which teach an enlarged Nicene faith, and which give the rich tapestry of Catholic beliefs, which must be in accord with this Creed and never contradict it.

This Creed came about as the result of Arianism, a heresy which denied the divinity of Jesus Christ and thus the Trinity. Arianism still exists today in varied forms — Unitarians, Jehovah's Witnesses, Mormons, for example, all of which are anti-Trinitarian. To refute these heretical beliefs, one must know them and know how to respond to them, and that is what this book is about.

If you are going to respond to the strangers at your door, you must be prepared to answer their claims and objections to your beliefs. To do this you must know more than a credal outline. There are a number of good adult catechisms available. Our Sunday Visitor, Inc., publishes *The Teachings of Christ* by Bishop Donald Wuerl, Father Ronald Lawler and Thomas Lawler (Huntington, Ind.). Father John Hardon has written the popular *The Catholic Catechism* (Doubleday, New York, 1975). A newer book is *The Church's Confession of Faith*, an adult catechism which is very complete, prepared under the auspices of the German hierarchy, systematically arranged, and most understandable (Ignatius Press, Harrison, N.Y.). One should have one of these or a similar volume in the home and be familiar with it.

In short, your witness to Jesus Christ will only be as good a your knowledge.

4

Key Scriptural Texts
You Should Know

HERE ARE SOME verses from the Bible concerning basic Catholic belief that could easily be committed to memory. They are grouped by topic, with a brief paragraph of commentary at the end of each, whenever necessary.

The Trinity

". . . Baptizing them in the name of the Father, and of the Son, and of the Holy Spirit. . ." (Mt 28:19).

The grace of the Lord Jesus Christ and the love of God and the fellowship of the Holy Spirit be with all of you (2 Cor 13:13).

The Trinity is a fundamental doctrine of Christianity. It unites the Churches of East and West, and even the Reformers held fast to it. It is one of the main sources of ecumenism. There are some sects and cults today that call themselves Christian, but in denying this basic teaching of Christianity, they refute their own claims.

Divinity of Jesus

"The Father and I are one" (Jn 10:30).

"Amen, Amen, I say to you, before Abraham came to be, I AM" (Jn 8:58).

In the Book of Exodus, when Moses asked God what His name was, God replied (3:14): "I am who am." Then He added, "This is what you shall tell the Israelites: 'I AM sent me to you.' " In applying this title to Himself, Jesus was declaring His total identity with God the Father, and was so understood by the Jews.

Establishment of a Church

"And I say to you, you are Peter, and upon this rock I will build my church, and the gates of the netherworld shall not prevail against it" (Mt 16:18).

In this statement Jesus clearly shows His intention to establish a Church of which Peter would be head. Since He also declared that this Church would endure to the end of time, the implication was that Peter would have successors. Hence, it becomes important to determine the Church Christ founded, not one founded by some man.

Power Given to Head of Church

"I will give you the keys of the kingdom of heaven. Whatever you bind on earth shall be bound in heaven; and whatever you loose on earth shall be loosed in heaven" (Mt 16:19).

This tremendous power was given to Peter and his successors.

Unity of the Church

"I have other sheep that do not belong to this fold. These also I must lead, and they will hear my voice, and there will be one flock, one shepherd" (Jn 10:16).

". . . So that they may all be one, as you, Father, are in me and I in you, that they also may be in us. . ." (Jn 17:21).

This call to unity is ever present. The large number of churches that exist, claiming to be Christ's but teaching various differences, is a scandal to the non-Christian world.

Baptism and Its Necessity

"Go, therefore, and make disciples of all the nations, baptizing them in the name of the Father, and of the Son, and of the Holy Spirit. . ." (Mt 28:19).

"Amen, Amen, I say to you, no one can enter the kingdom of God without being born of water and Spirit" (Jn 3:5).

"Whoever believes and is baptized will be saved; whoever does not believe will be condemned" (Mk 16:16).

It is on the basis of the above teachings that the Catholic Church practices infant baptism.

Purgatory

"Amen, I say to you, you will not be released until you have paid the last penny" (Mt 5:26).

Thus he made atonement for the dead that they might be freed from this sin (2 Mc 12:46).

Released, freed from where? Hell? Elsewhere, Scripture shows that Hell is a permanent and eternal state. Likewise, 2 Maccabees shows belief in a temporary place from which prayers and sacrifice can free those in sin.

Heaven and Hell

"Depart from me, you accursed, into the eternal fire prepared for the devil and his angels" (Mt 25:41).

"And these will go off to eternal punishment, but the righteous to eternal life" (Mt 25:46).

Eucharist

"Amen, Amen, I say to you, unless you eat the flesh of the Son of Man and drink his blood, you have no life within you. Whoever eats my flesh and drinks my blood has eternal life, and I will raise him on the last day. For my flesh is true food, and my blood is true drink." (Jn 6:53-55).

While they were eating, Jesus took bread, said the blessing, broke it, and giving it to his disciples said, "Take and eat; this is my body." Then he took a cup, gave thanks, and gave it to them, saying. "Drink from it, all of you, for this is my blood. . ." (Mt 26:26-28).

"Do this in memory of me" (Lk 22:19).

"Whoever eats my flesh and drinks my blood remains in me, and I in him" (Jn 6:56).

Therefore whoever eats the bread or drinks the cup of the Lord unworthily will have to answer for the body and blood of the Lord (1 Cor 11:27).

The Jews understood that Jesus was speaking literally and not symbolically, and that is why many left Him. The Eucharist is not a symbol but an ancient event taking place in the present moment.

Penance

"Receive the Holy Spirit. Whose sins you forgive are forgiven them; and whose sins you retain are retained" (Jn 20:22-23).

This authority was given by Jesus to His Church on the night of His Resurrection. It was a tremendous authority given to human beings (see Mt 9:8).

Confirmation

[Peter and John] went down and prayed for them that they might receive the Holy Spirit, for it had not yet fallen on any of them; they had only been baptized in the name of the Lord Jesus. Then they laid hands on them and they received the Holy Spirit (Acts 8:15-17).

Anointing of the Sick

Is there anyone among you sick? He should summon the presbyters of the church, and they should pray over him, anointing him with oil in the name of the Lord, and the prayer of faith will save the sick person, and the Lord will raise him up. If he has committed any sins, he will be forgiven (Jas 5:14-15).

Marriage

He said to them, "Whoever divorces his wife and marries another commits adultery against her, and if she divorces her husband and marries another, she commits adultery" (Mk 10:11-12).

How many churches today take this command of Christ literally?

The Blessed Virgin

". . . Behold, all ages from now on will call me blessed" (Lk 1:48).

"Hail, favored one! The Lord is with you.". . . "Most blessed are you among women" (Lk 1:28,42).

It is Scripture that calls Mary "blessed." She herself prophesied that she would be honored down the ages. The Catholic

Church has continually honored Mary for accepting to become the Mother of our Redeemer.

The verses above are key texts that should be familiar to every Catholic. There are other fundamental texts important to the development of Catholic theology, and they will be found in a good catechism. Many charges are placed against the Catholic Church by those unfamiliar with its doctrines and teaching. One frequently heard is that the Church is unbiblical and that its members are forbidden to read the Bible. The Catholic Church is entirely founded in Scripture, and nothing that it teaches can contradict the Bible. Unfortunately, many of those who make this charge and similar accusations are themselves guilty of selective use of the Bible, ignoring certain of the above texts because they do not agree with preconceived notions. The Church also places emphasis on its traditions, seeing the presence of the Holy Spirit in them, but even this tradition cannot be opposed to Scripture, in which the Church sees unconditional authority.

5

Some General Reminders

IN DISCUSSING matters of religion with those who come to your door or with those who stop you at an airport or other public place, certain things should be kept in mind. First, those who approach you have been trained in what they do. They know from experience what statements will be of interest. They have been drilled in scriptural texts that seemingly prove their statements. They have been rehearsed in answering the common objections put to them. Unless you know your own Faith well, you are at a disadvantage. To show these well-meaning people the falsity of their teachings, you must know what these teachings are and how to answer them.

Second, be aware that you may be using the same words but may not mean the same thing. For example, those who approach you may be talking about Jesus Christ but not mean the Jesus Christ of Christian Scripture. Jesus Christ for the Christian is one in nature with the Father, eternal, incarnated, who rose bodily from the dead and will return at the end of time to judge all humans. However, the Mormons interpret Jesus as a spirit brother of Lucifer, product of sexual intercourse between God and Mary, and only one of many gods. Jehovah's Witnesses see Jesus not as equal to the Father but as Jehovah's mightiest creation, who gave up his spirit life to become man, who did not rise bodily from the dead, and who did not atone for

27

all sins. The Moonies see Jesus as a failure whose mission is completed by the Lord of the Second Advent. Jehovah's Witnesses will talk to you about "resurrection" but the word is not used in the ordinary Christian sense; to them it means "re-creation" by God. It is well, therefore, at the beginning of discussion to define terms to be sure that you are both talking about the same things.

While the Christian Churches recognize the Bible as the source of their faith, these cultic sects need other books to explain their beliefs. The Mormons have the *Book of Mormon, Doctrine and Covenants, Pearl of Great Price*, and the collected teachings of their presidents, whom they regard as prophets. Jehovah's Witnesses use *Let God Be True*, a summary of Witness doctrines; *Make Sure of All Things*, Witness interpretation of scriptural passages, often taken out of context; and other Witness literature, such as *The Truth that Leads to Eternal Life*.

Third, use one of the newer and more accurate Bible translations that have been produced in recent years, such as the *New American Bible* or the *Revised Standard Version*. While the Douay Version and the King James Versions are held in great respect, their accuracy has been improved by modern scholarship. Do not argue with Jehovah's Witnesses using their translation of the Bible, *The New World Translation*, which is inaccurate and often biased.

For example John 1:1 is a key Christian Scripture. Both the *New American Bible*'s revised New Testament and the *Revised Standard Version* say: "In the beginning was the Word, and the Word was with God, and the Word was God." However, *The New World Translation* is: "In (the) beginning the Word was, and the Word was with God, and the Word was a god." You will note that the last usage of "God" is not capitalized and the article "a," which is not in the Greek, is inserted, contrary to Witness practice in their usage in similar Greek construction elsewhere in this same chapter. It is done to bolster up preconceived doctrinal teachings of the Witnesses.

There are many examples of this in their bible. The Witnesses have an explanation for this variance, but unfortunately for them it has no basis in fact. One of the difficulties with *The New World Translation* is that its translators are unknown and no one can check their credentials as translators. We do not have space to go into this matter in detail here, but there are scholarly critiques of the Witnesses' bible which the interested reader can find. All we wish to do here is alert the reader against using the bible of the Witnesses for any proofs of their teachings.

6

Jehovah's Witnesses

PRACTICALLY every family in the United States has had a visit from a Jehovah's Witness — a call made because the Witness believes it is necessary for his or her salvation. Each Witness is considered a minister, and all are mobilized to evangelize a given area, house by house, selling their publications and offering Bible studies under Witness guidance.

Because of civil court cases, many people are aware that the Witnesses oppose blood transfusions and saluting of the flag. But they seem to be against more things than those they are for. William J. Whalen, who has studied the group, writes in his book *Separated Brethren*: "Compared to Jehovah's Witnesses, Calvin Coolidge's minister who declared himself against sin was a piker. The Witnesses oppose blood transfusions, business, Catholics, Christmas trees, communism, civic enterprises, the doctrines of hell and immortality, evolution, flag saluting, higher education, liquor, Protestants, priests, the pope, public office, military service, movies, Mother's Day, religion, Sunday schools, the Trinity, tobacco, the United Nations, voting, the Y.M.C.A., Wall Street, and women's rights. This list does not pretend to be complete."

Witness headquarters are in Brooklyn, New York, where they have a highly developed center of church offices, publishing and printing plant, and dormitories for Witnesses who give their time to publishing, printing, and distribution of Witness magazines and books in return for room and board, clothing, and a small living allowance. There is a fulfillment operation in Wallkill, New York. The main Witness magazine is *The Watchtower*, which is devoted to "announcing Jehovah's Kingdom," with each semi-monthly printing averaging over twelve million copies and printed in 103 languages. An alternating semi-monthly magazine is *Awake!*, which gives the Witness view on world affairs and concerns, and averages about 10 million copies an issue in 53 languages. In addition, the publishing house turns out scores of tracts and such books as the *New World Translation of Holy Scriptures* and doctrinal works such as *Let God Be True, Qualified to Be Ministers, Make Sure of All Things, Life Everlasting, The Truth That Leads to Everlasting Life* (totaling now about 60 million copies), etc. The sect does not operate any works of charity, but it does have a Bible school in its Columbia Heights headquarters in Brooklyn which trains students in the Witness bible and prepares them for foreign service.

Along with the Mormons, the Witnesses are a fast-growing cult. In 1945, with the end of World War II and with male Witnesses coming out of jails for refusing to serve in the armed forces, the cult claimed 141,606 members, having actually doubled during the war years. Today they number well over two million, with 600,000 in the United States. They also have a considerable number of fellow-travelers who subscribe to Witness teachings but are unprepared to sacrifice their time as the organization demands.

The Beginnings

The Witness cult began with Charles Taze Russell, who was born in 1852 in Pittsburgh (Allegheny), Pennsylvania, and at the age of fifteen went to work in his father's clothing stores. Originally a Presbyterian, he switched as a boy to the Congregational Church, but by the age of seventeen had become disillusioned with its biblical interpretation, despite the fact that he had no real education himself. In 1870 he came in contact with a group of Adventists whom he found more to his liking, ultimately rejecting them because they taught that Jesus would return to earth in the flesh, and he believed the Second Coming would be invisible. He gathered a few friends to meet with him for Bible studies under his tutelage.

In 1876 Russell learned of a disaffected group of Adventists who met in Rochester under the leadership of H. N. Barbour. The two groups became allied, and Russell and Barbour published a book, *Three Worlds or Plan of Redemption*, which asserted that the Second Coming had begun invisibly and that the Gentile times would end in 1914. However, in 1879 Russell disagreed with other Barbour teachings. He broke away and started his own periodical, *Zion's Watch Tower*, which was to be the basis of the movement's growth. Other congregations were organized, and in 1884 Zion's Watch Tower Tract Society was incorporated with Russell at its head. The purpose of the Society was the dissemination of Russell's biblical teachings through printed matter in various languages. Thus began an unending flood of literature from the Allegheny headquarters, all concerned with Russell's personal but uneducated conclusions, focusing on the end of the world.

Russell also traveled widely promoting the movement. In 1903 a branch was set up in Germany, and the following year in Australia. Joseph Franklin Rutherford, a Missouri lawyer, became legal counsel for the Society, and in 1908 he obtained property for the group in Brooklyn, New York, incorporating there the following year under the title People's Pulpit Association, which was not changed to its present name until 1956. Russell, however, was not immune to trouble. His wife sued him for divorce on the grounds of "his conceit, egotism, domination, and improper conduct in relation to other women."

Russell used his publications to promote pet ideas — a miracle cure for cancer made from chloride of zinc, a Millennial bean, a marvelous cottonseed, and a miracle wheat at a dollar a pound, which he claimed would grow five times faster than ordinary grain. The Brooklyn *Daily Eagle* ridiculed his claims, particularly of the wheat, and when the paper published a satirical cartoon of Pastor Russell and his wheat, he sued for libel. When the defense introduced a government report which showed that the wheat instead of being "five times as good" was inferior to ordinary wheat, he lost the case. In another case, in which he sued a Canadian Baptist pastor, Russell was shown to be a perjurer. When asked if he knew Greek, he replied affirmatively, but when challenged to read the Greek letters at the top of a page of the Greek Testament, he was unable. Although he also claimed to have been ordained, he was forced to admit in this trial that he never was. Again he lost a suit. Russell died in 1916, aboard a Pullman car in Pampa, Texas, returning from California. He requested an aide to dress him in a Roman toga, "drew up his feet like Jacob of old," and expired.

Continued Growth

Russell was succeeded as president by "Judge" Joseph F. Rutherford, the Society's lawyer, who began debunking some of Russell's more flagrant claims. This resulted in several groups breaking away. Rutherford, who preferred to write rather than sermonize, began a long list of publications he was to author. He also involved the members of the cult in door-to-door sales. He recorded talks which the Witnesses played on a phonograph during house calls. Rutherford found himself in legal trouble like his predecessor. In Canada, Watchtower publications were banned on grounds of sedition. When the United States entered World War I, Rutherford and seven associates were arrested and tried on charges of conspiracy and refusal to serve in the armed forces. They were found guilty and sentenced to the federal penitentiary in Atlanta. With the end of the war, Witnesses petitioned their congressmen for release of their leaders, and as a result the sentence was reversed and the leaders were freed.

Rutherford was to direct the sect for a quarter century, dividing his time between the Brooklyn headquarters and a California mansion he had bought in the name of Abel, Noah, and Abraham, who he said would return before the Battle of Armageddon. Rutherford converted the Society into a theocracy in which local leaders would no longer be elected but appointed by him. He also gave the group a new name — Jehovah's Witnesses. He expanded the printing operation, replaced Russell's books and tracts with his own, and changed the emphasis for salvation from Bible studies to witnessing — house calls and selling literature. Rutherford, after his release from Atlanta, had coined a slogan that was heavily promoted by the Witnesses: "Millions Now Living Will Never Die." Unfortunately, he was not one of them. He passed away January 8, 1942.

Rutherford was succeeded by Nathan H. Knorr, who had left the Reformed Church in Pennsylvania as a teenager to become a Witness. He worked his way up through the hierarchy, becoming the printing manager, a director, and vice-president. Knorr was to author textbooks which have become standard lesson material for the Witnesses. He supervised *The New World Translation of the Christian Greek Scriptures*, released in parts and then made into a Bible in 1961, with some changes from previous parts. It has never been divulged who did this translation, and Witness literature claims the translators have requested to remain anonymous, even after their deaths. Some Scripture scholars suspect that the work is but a rephrasing of other Protestant translations and did not really use Greek sources.

In a Scottish court case, Frederick Franz had to state under oath that he was one of the translators. His educational background was two years at the University of Cincinnati. Anthony A. Hoekema, a seminary professor of systematic theology, who has studied the Witnesses, has written: "Their *New World*

Translation of the Bible is by no means an objective rendering of the sacred text into modern English but is a biased translation in which many of the peculiar teachings of the Watchtower Society are smuggled into the text of the Bible itself."

It was Franz who was to succeed Knorr when the latter died in 1972, becoming the first Witness leader to have had any college training. This lack of education of Witness leadership has given the movement an anti-intellectualism that appeals to others who have not gone beyond high school. It also makes for docile recruits who are unwilling to question the teachings of their leadership. Franz's presidency has been marked by international growth.

What Witnesses Teach

In order to refute the Witnesses, one must know what they teach and how these teachings diverge from the doctrines of the recognized Christian churches.

God

"What, then, do the facts show as to the 'Trinity'?" asks a Witness study text, *The Truth That Leads to Eternal Life.* "Neither the word nor the idea is in God's Word, the Bible. The doctrine did not originate with God." Adds another text, *Let God Be True,* "The obvious conclusion is, therefore, that Satan is the originator of the Trinity doctrine." According to the Witnesses, there is only one person in God, Jehovah, a name they render from the Hebrew *Yahweh* and substitute some 235 times for the Greek usage of Lord (*Kyrios*) and God (*Theos*) in the New Testament. The Witnesses accuse Christians of borrowing the idea of a trinity from Babylonian, Hindu, and Egyptian paganism, or what they call "demon religions." According to their teaching, Jesus is not a divine person and the Holy Spirit does not even exist but is, as *Let God Be True* says, "the invisible active force of Almighty God which moves his servants to do his will."

The Witnesses do not believe in divine mystery, and their Jehovah is simple to figure out and understand. They assign to Jehovah the attributes of power, wisdom, justice, and love. They see their god as an avenger who is in constant struggle for sovereignty of the earth. They repeat this idea of God as vindicator throughout their literature. Beyond the four mentioned above, nothing is said about other attributes of God, which include His omnipotence, immensity, incomprehensibility, infinity, simplicity, spiritual substance, and transcendence. They make the basic mistake of thinking that God can be comprehended by the human mind, that the infinite can be contained in the finite.

However, Witness arguments can confuse the Christians who have not been educated in their religion. "If Jesus and the Father are one," they ask, "how could Jesus pray to Himself in the Garden? Or how could He send Himself to earth to be born?" They say that Christians believe that Jesus is the Father, which is of course not true. They accuse Christians of having a fractured God, one-third Father, one-third Son, and one-third Holy Spirit; their god is wholly one. "You tell me three is one," they say, "and this is unreasonable. If it is against reason, it is wrong. Doesn't Isaiah (1:18) say, 'Come now and let us reason together, saith the LORD'? That's all I'm asking you to do is be reasonable." What the Witness is doing here is making a play on words, as if they meant the same thing, and also taking Isaiah out of the legal context in which he is speaking. The revised *New American Bible* translation, "Come now, let us set things right, says the LORD," more correctly brings out the Hebrew meaning. Here again we see the danger of using a poor translation of Scripture.

Moreover, the Witness will tell the Christians whom he is seeking to convert that the Trinity is a man-made doctrine, since the word is never mentioned in the Bible. There are many

words and phrases in Christian usage that are described in the
Bible as is the Trinity but not specifically named. Original sin is
a good example. The fall of Adam is never called original sin in
the text, but that is the name we give it. When Jesus gives the
Trinity formula in Matthew 28:19, He is describing the Trinity
without putting a name to it.

Jesus Christ

According to Witness doctrine (*Let God Be True*), Jesus
Christ is nothing more than "a perfect man; and not the Supreme God Almighty." According to *The Kingdom Is at Hand*,
Jesus is "the first and direct creation of Jehovah God." To support this position they have had to mistranslate John 1:1 in
their Bible. If you will consult any recognized translation you
will read: "In the beginning was the Word, and the Word was
with God, and the Word was God." However, the Witnesses
render this text: "In the beginning the Word was, and the
Word was with God, and the Word was a god." Thus the *New
World Translation* lower-cases "God," referring to Jesus, and
introduces the indefinite article "a," which is not in the Greek.

The Greek for "Word" is *Logos*. John uses *logos* as a syno-
nym for Jesus Christ. The Witnesses, however, use *logos* to
mean "spokesman" for Jehovah God. He was in effect the chief
executive officer for God who communicated with the angels
and the rest of creation. After He was created by God, Jesus was
in effect an angel, known as Michael the Archangel. The Witnesses attributed three states to Jesus: pre-human as an angel,
human as man, post-human as a risen spirit. When Jesus became man, He was divested of His angelic nature. The Witnesses see death as an annihilation of the body. Thus the body of
Jesus was destroyed in death and His Second Coming will be as
pure spirit, hence invisible. The Witnesses lift scriptural texts
from context to bolster their arguments. Yet the Risen Christ
claims that He is not a ghost but has flesh and bones (Lk 24:39),

and He asks Thomas to feel His body (Jn 20:24-29). The Witnesses explained these texts by saying Jesus temporarily materialized a body, just as angels did when they appeared as men.

The implications of Witness teachings about Jesus Christ and His sacrifice are many and involved. It could not have had infinite value, as Christians teach, because Jesus Christ was but man. It was not universal because those who were annihilated in death, like Adam, remain annihilated. God did not send His only-begotten Son to redeem man, but a sinless man whom God caused to be conceived by Mary as a human son.

The Holy Spirit

The Holy Spirit is not a person but an active force emanating from God, something like electricity, or as the Witness book *Let Your Name Be Sanctified* defines it, the Holy Spirit "is the impersonal, invisible active force that finds its source and reservoir in Jehovah God and that he uses to accomplish his will even at great distances over light years of space." Thus the Holy Spirit is neither God nor person. In John 14:16 Jesus calls the Holy Spirit Advocate (*Paraklētos*) and what Jesus describes is a person who can reason and counsel. Jesus refers to the Paraclete as "Him" and "He," meaning a person, not some impersonal force or power of God. There are many texts in Scripture that depict the personality of the Holy Spirit. John 14, 15, and 16 show the Holy Spirit at work. In Acts 10:19 and 13:2 He is a directing Spirit. St. Paul's theology of the Holy Spirit, as shown in his letters, contradicts the teachings of the Witnesses.

Salvation

The Witnesses limit heaven to 144,000 anointed souls, a figure arrived at through a misinterpretation of Revelation 7:4. They take the number literally and ignore Jewish symbolism for which it stands (12 x 12 x 1,000): the number 12 stands for perfection in the human world, the second 12 represents the 12 tribes of Israel and 1,000 is another symbolic number indicating not an actual figure but a very large number. Revelation's use of 144,000 only means a vast number, not the literal figure of the Witnesses.

The Witnesses adopted this number early, and as long as the cult was small and struggling, inclusion was something to be sought. However, now that the Witnesses far exceed this number and most Witnesses cannot gain the heavenly kingdom, they have been told they will be given new bodies and enjoy perfect happiness in the coming earthly paradise; they obtain this right not through the sacrifice of Christ but by being faithful to their duties as Witnesses on earth. One wonders why members of the sect endure this division of "anointed" and "sheep" and the loss of earthly heaven by so many "sheep." The only answer is that the Witnesses accept without question or discrimination what their leaders have taught them.

The Sacraments and Sacramentals

Baptism. All converts must be baptized by immersion, even if previously baptized, thus indicating that the Witnesses do not see baptism imprinting a permanent mark on the soul. While the formula sounds Christian, it really is not: "In the name of the Father and of the Son and of the holy spirit." Since their baptismal form is anti-trinitarian and since they are not baptizing in the name of the Trinity as Jesus taught, their baptism is invalid.

For the Christian, baptism is a sign of faith by which one turns his or her whole life toward Jesus Christ and an entry into His Church. It is the foundation of ecumenical communion, since the Catholic Church recognizes any baptism that uses the formula of Jesus and makes use of water, either by immersion or by pouring. Among the effects of baptism is the forgiveness of sin, the gift of new life in Christ, and the imprint of an indelible spiritual mark on the soul of the person baptized, marking such a person as specially dedicated to God.

The Witnesses, on the other hand, see baptism as only something symbolic of one's dedication to be Jehovah's minister. In *Make Sure of All Things* baptism is described as "an outward symbol, as a testimony before witnesses, of the baptized one's complete, unreserved and unconditional dedication and agreement to do the will of Jehovah." The Witnesses do not recognize the baptism that may have been previously received by their converts, do not recognize infant baptism, and accept only baptism by immersion. There is also a "baptism of the holy spirit [sic]" administered by Jesus Christ to Jehovah's anointed (the 144,000) and a baptism of the Greater Noah, which is described in *You May Survive Armageddon* as "baptism into Jesus Christ." The baptism of the Greater Noah is for the sheep (not the 144,000) and will enable them to survive Armageddon as long as they continue to serve Jehovah.

Eucharist. The other sacrament which the Witnesses give a nod to is the Lord's Supper which they call the Memorial and celebrate once a year after sunset according to their own calendar (Abib or Nisan 14, "the true passover date of the Jews"), which approximates Easter but can fall on any day of the week. Unleavened bread and fermented wine make up the Memorial but are only symbols of Christ's body and blood. The Memorial is meant only for the anointed and not the sheep, although the latter are encouraged to attend. While Christ meant this sacrament for all His followers, the Witnesses restrict it to their elite.

Odd Ideas

Man. The main doctrine that the Witnesses propagate about man is that man has no immortal soul. He ceases to exist after death but will be recreated from God's memory at the time of the resurrection. They ignore scriptural texts that contradict their teaching, e.g., Ecclesiastes 12:7: "The dust returns to the earth as it once was, and the life breath returns to God who gave it"; or Jesus' description of the Last Judgment (Mt 25:46 and preceding) when He speaks of the soul going to eternal life or punishment.

Government. *Let God Be True* tells the members of the cult: "Since their allegiance is to Almighty God and his kingdom they do not participate in local, national or international election or politics." The same book forbids Witnesses to fulfill military obligations, saying to do so would make them deserters of Jehovah. Finally, *Let God Be True* gives the admonition: "Jehovah's witnesses do not salute the flag of any nation." However, such commands are contrary to the teaching of Jesus, who told us to give to Caesar the things that belonged to Caesar and advised us to be a leaven in our society. St. Paul in Romans 13 tells Christians that they must be obedient to authority and to look upon civil authority as exercising God's power. Once again the Witnesses ignore Scripture that contradicts their founders' pet ideas, and it is an example of how they cut themselves off from society and then blame society for persecuting them. However, the Witnesses will use society's structures when it benefits them, e.g., civil suits brought by the sect.

Blood Transfusions. For a Witness to accept a blood transfusion would be "at the cost of eternal life." Witnesses root this teaching in a complete misunderstanding of Genesis 9:4: "Flesh with its lifeblood still in it you shall not eat." To understand this biblical prohibition, you must understand the Semitic mind and the times in which it was written. The Semitic concept was that blood was the seat of life and hence sacred. This is why Genesis and Leviticus make their prohibition against eating blood. It has nothing to do with blood transfusions, which were unknown until our own time. The Semitic teaching that blood had to be drained from any meat finds its echo in kosher practices today, but no Jew is opposed to blood transfusions on these grounds.

Holidays. Witness teaching-literature labels both Christmas and Easter "of pagan origin," hence they are not to be celebrated. They also oppose birthday celebrations as "worshiping a person." It is true that Christmas is an artificial feast because we do not know what day Jesus was born. Some scholars think it may even have been in the spring of the year. It is a date the Catholic Church chose arbitrarily to commemorate Christ's birth. The date chosen did replace a pagan feast of the winter solstice, but the new feast was a Christian feast with the aim of drawing people away from a pagan celebration. This is a common practice in Church history, and a modern example occurred when Pope Pius XII in 1955 wanted to draw Christians away from the communist celebration of May Day. He instituted the new Feast of St. Joseph the Worker and ordered it to be celebrated on May 1 (May Day), but this does not make it a communist feast.

Easter is another story. Again it is true that pagans held fertility rites in the spring, but Easter has nothing to do with them, even as a replacement. Easter is celebrated in connection with the Jewish Passover, the period in which Christ died. The Jewish feast goes back to the Exodus, when the Jews were freed from the Egyptian yoke and were able to escape to freedom. To suggest that it is of pagan origin shows only a bias and lack of knowledge.

Birthdays seem so peripheral to the important deviations of the Witnesses that they hardly seem worth talking about, yet their celebration is condemned in *The Truth That Leads to Eternal Life* because "they exalt the creature, making him the center of attention rather than the Creator." Certainly, there is nothing in the Bible that forbids commemorating birthdays or holidays, and the prohibition is but another example of the joyless aberrations of the cult.

One can well ask how people can come to accept such twisted interpretations of Scripture. The answer is in the type of convert the Witnesses get — undiscriminating, susceptible to suggestion, and easily led. In recent years the cult has made organized efforts to recruit blacks, Puerto Ricans, and Mexican-Americans, with considerable success. These minorities, largely uneducated and untrained in their previous religions, have proven a fertile ground for Witness proselytizing.

The Witness leadership claims to be the wise servant ("faithful and prudent") whom Jehovah has appointed over His human family (Mt 24:45), and repeated insistence on this fact becomes ingrained in the convert. It was Charles Russell, the founder, who came up with this principle. At first he called all the Watchtower membership the servant, but his wife pointed out the word was singular and applied only to him, so adopted that interpretation. After his death he continued to be the "wise servant" until Judge Rutherford in 1927 dethroned him and made the congregation, acting through its membership, the servant. Thus even Watchtower prophets can be wrong.

It wasn't the only time that their prophets mixed up God's will. One need only go back into Witness literature — *Zion's Watch Tower, The Time Is at Hand, Millions Living Will Never Die*, etc. — and find their failures in predicting the end of the world. Russell said clearly the final battle of Armageddon would take place in 1914. When this didn't happen, the prediction was corrected to 1925 and, when that failed, to 1975. The Witnesses maintain that these dates are definitely fixed in Scripture and, since Christ's Second Coming was invisible, they cannot be proven wrong. Yet Matthew 24:30 specifically says all tribes of the earth shall see the Son of Man coming with much power and majesty. The same chapter warns of false prophets (vv. 5 and 23), while this chapter and others (Mk 13:32; Lk 12:40) insist that no man knows the day and hour when the Second Coming will take place, texts the Witnesses ignore.

While the Witnesses claim the Bible to be the infallible word of God that must be followed, they make the Bible meaningless by their queer interpretations of it. Perhaps the fault is in the lack of scholars in the organization. They have a few people who are supposedly self-educated but who have no recognition from competent authorities. They have no leaders in their membership from the fields of education, politics, science, business, letters, or the military. But this hardly matters to them. The Witness leadership has such a hold over its membership that their teachings are accepted without question, no matter how absurd they appear to the educated mind of an outsider.

At the same time one must look upon the ordinary Witness with great respect and sadness. The Witness's whole social and religious life revolves around Kingdom Hall and its activities. One's free time is not free but must be spent at Kingdom Hall at Watchtower lectures, study of the Bible and of Witness literature, service meetings, Theocratic Ministry School, witnessing, and selling literature. It is a closed society that the convert enters, one which demands his total dedication. If he balks, he is expelled and shunned by the community, even his own family. The pressure to conform is very heavy.

Conclusions

In a short book like this it is impossible to go into all of the Witness teachings, some of which are quite involved and take devious turns through both Scripture and reason. What we have tried to show here are basic Witness principles that deviate from ordinary Christianity, and that Witness arguments can be answered by one familiar with his or her own faith and with Bible teachings. In dealing with Witnesses who come to your door, certain truths should be kept in mind:

1. Don't accept something at face value, simply because someone says it is so. Ask questions. What do you mean by

that? How does that jibe with such and such a teaching in the Bible?

2. Don't even accept words at face value. When you are dealing with a Witness, you may be using the same words, but they have very different meanings — words such as God or Jesus Christ, and terms such as Holy Spirit (Witnesses do not even capitalize this) or Second Coming. It is a good principle of logic that in any discussion the participants define the terms that are being used. Just as you can misunderstand words used by the Witness, the Witness in turn can misunderstand you. For example, Witnesses call themselves Christians, although they deny all the basic Christian doctrines. At the same time they do not consider you a Christian but a member of a demonic cult they are seeking to save.

3. Treat the stranger at your door with Christian charity and see in him an opportunity to win a soul to Christ and His Church. You may disagree, but never become disagreeable. However, if your argument becomes too much for a Witness, he or she will probably retreat to Kingdom Hall and its overseer for an answer.

4. Do not use the Witness's Bible but one of the scholarly and accepted translations. Encourage the Witness to examine the context in which a text is placed and compare it with similar references. Witnesses really do not know the Bible but rely on selected texts that appear in Witness literature.

5. Try to find out why the Witness became a Witness. The answer may give you a cue on how to proceed. Many Witnesses were former Catholics. Ask them how they could give up the Eucharist and other sacraments, suffer the loss of their saints and their holy days, and enter a church founded not by Jesus Christ but by a man.

6. Above all, if you are going to enter into a conversation with this stranger at your door, remember, if you do not know your own Faith well, the Witness may persuade you to his. I be-

lieve more converts are made from ignorance than any other cause.

7. If the conversation lags, ask the Witness to pray with you. You will find that he does not want to do that and will quickly leave.

8. Finally, be aware that the key doctrine that separates you from the Witness is the doctrine of the Trinity: the one un-created God in three distinct persons. The Trinity is the founda-tion of Christian faith, and thus no one can deny it and remain a Christian.

Some Obligations You May Meet

Witnesses are trained in certain charges against the main-line churches and will often use them if the conversation goes on long enough. You should be prepared to answer them.

Jesus gave two great commandments: love of God and love of one's fellowman. He even said one should love his enemy. The history of Christianity is a history of continuous warfare, of Christian killing Christian. This applies to Catholics and Prot-estants. Jehovah's Witnesses will not go to war and kill Chris-tian brothers.

There are really two questions here. One about the failure of Christian churches and the second about a just war. The best answer to the first is: I admit that there have been failures over the centuries, that men have continually failed God. It hap-pened among the Apostles and continues to this day. But that doesn't mean that the teachings of Christ which the Church holds are wrong. We don't throw the baby out with the bath-water. We work to convert the Church members to the teach-ings of Jesus. You are looking for perfection, and it will not be found in this life. As for wars, a nation has the right to protect itself from an unjust aggressor, the same as an individual. A witness would not be condemned by his own for resisting an aggressor against his family or home.

St. Paul says in 1 Corinthians 1:10 that there should be no divisions among Christians, that they should be of one mind and judgment. What do we find? Arguments over doctrines. Fights between conservatives and progressives. Get a group of mixed Christians together and see if the individuals in the group agree on the Bible.

This is called the scandal of a divided Christianity, and it is against the will of Jesus, who prayed for unity. The ecumenical movement is a step in correcting this, seeking areas on which agreement can be found, building on those, and respecting the sincere belief of others. There are many churches. But Jesus did found a Church that He said would endure until the end of the world. Again, you should be searching among those Christian churches to discover which Church Jesus founded.

What about the Inquisition?

Which Inquisition? The Spanish Inquisition or the Roman Inquisition? The Spanish Inquisition was an instrument of the Spanish crown and was as much political as religious. The Spanish monarchy believed it was being undermined by Moors (Muslims) and Jews who insincerely converted to Catholicism but practiced their own faiths. As the *New Columbia Encyclopedia* points out, "The popes were never reconciled to the institution, which they regarded as usurping the church's prerogative." The tortures and trials of this Inquisition were notorious, but we must remember most of the accounts of it are from the English, mortal enemies of Spain. The Spanish Inquisition cannot be justified in light of modern morality, but this was another time when cruelty was more general. The Spanish crown believed it was defending itself and used the methods of the time with many abuses. But don't blame the Church for what Ferdinand and Isabella started. The Roman Inquisition was in the Middle Ages and was pretty much localized to southern France against the Albigensians. It was the ultimate application of Matthew 10:28. However, Church sentences were not generally severe, and what abuses there were came from secular rulers. The Church inquisitors wanted to win back the heretic, not punish him. Look these Inquisitions up in an objective history and interpret them in the light of their times.

The Catholic Church had an agreement with Hitler not to interfere with Nazi politics. This led to the deaths of millions of Jews.

Again, there are two accusations here. The fact is that the Church did excommunicate Nazis, and the papal encyclical of Pope Pius XI that was ordered read in all churches (*Mit Brennender Sorge*) did condemn Nazi racial policies. After it was read, priests were rounded up and sent to concentration camps. Thousands of Catholic priests died in these Nazi torture chambers. As for helping Jews, in 1941 *The New York Times* reported that Pope Pius XII was "about the only ruler left on the continent of Europe who dares to raise his voice at all . . . against Hitlerism." When Pius XII died, Jewish leaders credited him with rescuing 800,000 Jews from Nazi death camps. You are simply repeating the big lie without investigating the facts.

I have read that Catholics were punished and put to death for reading the Bible.

Can you cite me a case or two, because I have never heard of one? I thought you were going to say Catholics chained the Bible so that it couldn't be read. That was true in medieval times, but not so that it couldn't be read. You must remember, in those days most people could not read or write, and the Bible had to be read to them. It was kept on a rostrum in the church and chained there so it could not be removed. Before the advent of printing, a Bible had to be hand-copied — a tedious and ex pensive job. What copies there were had to be protected from theft.

In John 17, Jesus says that neither He nor His followers can be part of this world. This means we must be neutral toward politics, as Jehovah's Witnesses are.

It doesn't mean that at all. Jesus was talking about the spirit and "wisdom" of the world — its values — which are the direct antithesis of His teachings. He told us that we have to be in the world but not of it; that is, we cannot accept the values of the world. Jesus did not tell us to retreat from the world but to be a leaven in it, a city on a mountaintop. He commanded that we render to Caesar what is Caesar's but give to God what is God's. Paul even recommends that we pray for civil authority (1 Tm 2:2) because, as it says elsewhere, all authority comes from God. Paul recognized the structures of his time and even sent an escaped slave back to his master (Phlm 10-12).

There is no scriptural principle for a clergy class, particularly a paid one. Jesus told His followers not to charge for their services. Paul supported himself by his own work. Jehovah's Witnesses follow the scriptural teachings.

Again you are mixing up a lot of questions. Jesus founded a Church and selected Apostles to lead that Church. He set Peter over the Apostles to lead them and confirm their faith. If you know anything about the early Church, you must know there was a clergy class — read the letters to Timothy and Titus. This was not a new idea, for there was a priestly class blessed by God in the Old Testament. As for support, Jesus told His disciples to accept support because a laborer was worthy of his hire. Paul did support himself, but read all of 1 Corinthians 9, not a selected verse or two. He does not insist others be like him and defends their right to support for themselves and even their wives. Priests, ministers, and rabbis spend full time at their religious tasks and have the right to support.

Christians avoid using God's name. Read John 17:26,
where Jesus says His followers will declare the name of God.

I presume you are speaking of Jehovah, a non-word invented for the authorized version. In the Hebrew Bible the
name of God is written with its four consonants YHWH,
Yahweh, which the Jews held sacred as a name and did not pro-
nounce but substituted *Adonai* (Lord) or simply called it the
"name." The New Testament authors followed this practice.
The origin of "Yahweh" is uncertain; modern scholars associate it with the verb *hawah*, an archaic form of the verb "to
be." Biblical scholarship has advanced considerably since 1611
when the King James version was issued. The sacred name in
the New Testament is that of Jesus, at the mention of which,
Paul tells us (Phil 2:10), every knee in heaven and on earth
should bend.

Jesus said His main objective was to preach about the King-
dom of God. Jehovah's Witnesses do this, not the Christian
churches. The future of mankind is in God's real government,
the Kingdom, with Jesus as King.

Jesus alternated between Kingdom of God and Kingdom of
Heaven. He was not preaching a worldly kingdom, and this is
what the Apostles expected before the Resurrection. Jehovah's
Witnesses are making the same mistake. Jesus said specifically
that His kingdom was not of this world (Jn 18:36). The kingdom phrase is popular with the synoptic Gospels but not John.
Mark and Luke prefer the Kingdom of God expressions and it
is found thirty-one times in Luke and fourteen in Mark, but
only three times in Matthew, who prefers the Jewish expression
"Kingdom of Heaven"; the Jews used "heaven" as a reverential
term for God. Matthew uses it thirty times. Actually the translation "kingdom" for the Greek *basilea* and its Semitic equal
would be better translated as "reign" or "kingship." We have
to examine these expressions in context to get their full theological significance.

The examples above are not all-inclusive but cite a few objections that Witnesses use. Their aim is to put you on the defensive, and if you cannot respond to their objections to Christianity, they will press on with their claims about their own group, reasoning that you will be unable to dispute those. If you do answer their early accusations, they may listen to your explanation of why you are a Christian. In short, the more you know about your own religion, the better you will be able to explain it to others.

7

The Mormons
(Church of Jesus Christ
of Latter-Day Saints)

I MET MY first Mormon many years ago, and I was deeply impressed by him. It was in the days of propeller-driven airliners when seating was only four across — two and two, with an aisle in between. I was flying from San Francisco to Seattle, and a young lad sat next to me, about fourteen years old. We began talking, as people did in those days, and he told me that his parents were sending him on a trip to visit relatives before he died.

"Before you die?" I involuntarily exclaimed.

"Yes," he replied simply. "I have leukemia."

There was a moment of silence because I didn't know what to say, and, as if realizing my confused thoughts and feelings, he went on: "I'm not afraid to die because I know I will be exalted. There's only one thing I am sad about."

"And that is . . .?"

"I will not be able to undertake a mission like every Mormon should."

We talked about other things, but over the years this young man's frustrated zeal has stayed with me, because I considered him a model for Christian behavior. At the time, beyond the Mormon Tabernacle Choir, I knew nothing about Mormons, so I set out to find out more and I continued to be impressed. I learned that the Mormons were hardworking people whose lives revolved around the family. They were patriotic and led good, moral lives. They did not believe in becoming a burden to the state but through cooperation took care of the wants of their own who needed welfare.

My admiration for their zeal was not lessened in the years to come when I saw them in pairs, always recognizable, riding bicycles down a dusty Filipino road, walking the streets of an Andean village, or going from house to house in the United States. It wasn't until I examined the doctrines and teachings of this sect, which many authorities refer to as a cult, that I came to the conclusion that underneath a pleasant surface the Mormons were strange indeed and certainly not the Christians they claimed to be.

Today more people are familiar with Mormons. Many families have been visited by their young priest-elders seeking converts. They are the subjects of a good press which reports on their fine activities — coming together to save a city from a flood, feeding their needy after a disastrous harvest. Their college football and basketball teams have proven to be strong competitors and gained many non-Mormon followers. Unlike the Witnesses, they number leading Americans among their followers — senators, representatives, governors, college presidents, scientists, business executives, writers. Their clever and effective radio and television advertising in behalf of strong family life is both impressive and effective. In short, they are as wholesome as motherhood and apple pie. But if you thought that the doctrines of Jehovah's Witnesses in the preceding section were esoteric, wait until you meet the Mormons, who present one face to the world and quite another to their initiates.

The Mormons, or more properly, the Church of Jesus Christ of Latter Day Saints (LDS), have their headquarters in Salt Lake City, Utah, and pretty much control that state. They are also numerous in Idaho, California, and other Western states. Mormonism began with two men, Joseph Smith and Oliver Cowdery, when, according to Smith, "In May of 1829 we went into the woods to pray. While we were praying, a heavenly messenger, who identified himself as John the Baptist, descended and conferred upon both Oliver and myself the priesthood of Aaron." The following year in Fayette, New York, the church was organized and incorporated with six members. Today the Mormon Church has grown to four million members nationally and several million overseas. It is probably the wealthiest church in the world, exercising enormous economic power, owning hotels, motels, newspapers, radio and television stations, insurance companies, ranches (300,000 acres in Florida), factories, office buildings, department stores, a sugar plantation, a refinery in Ohio, utilities, factories, farms, office buildings, and even a tourist attraction (the Polynesian Cultural Center in Hawaii). The annual income of the sect is estimated at over a billion dollars a year. Although born and nurtured in persecution (which still has an effect today in the Mormon psyche), the sect has become both a financial and political power. Mormon membership grows by 250,000 each year, and the worldwide total is 6.5 million. There are 16,000 congregations in the United States alone.

Is Mormonism a Cult?

A number of writers on the Church of Latter-Day Saints have labeled it a cult. Robert and Grechen Passantino, in their "Answers to the Mormons," write: "Historically, Mormonism has been considered a cult because its primary teachings are completely opposed to the cardinal teachings of the Bible, reflected in Christian church history." However, deviation from the Bible does not, at least to this writer, seem to be a primary mark of a cult. Islam, Buddhism, and Hinduism are all accepted religions in which the Bible is not an operative book. Cults have been defined as everything from "organized heresy" to "a nonhistorical movement that promotes an ecstatic consciousness."

It would seem that there are almost as many definitions of a cult as there are writers.

However, in studying literature on cults certain marks seem to stand out in them:

Authoritarian — revolving around a strong personality who is the final authority.

Oppositional — rejecting recognized authority and its teachings.

Exclusive — promoting its membership as an elite group which alone has the truth.

Esoteric — teaching odd doctrines of its guru or prophet which are alien to main-line religions.

Sanction-Oriented — maintaining strict discipline rooted in group pressure and disfellowship.

Persecution-Conscious — promoting the idea that its members are subject to misunderstanding and persecution for their ideas.

Missionary Zeal — prepared to make sacrifices of money, effort, and time to promote their beliefs; convert-making, fund-raising and indoctrination take a disproportionate amount of time.

On the basis of the above list, the Church of Latter-Day Saints would appear to be a cult, since it possesses all of the marks. But then so too would the Roman world have regarded early Christianity as a cult descended from Judaism. A pertinent question seems to be then: When does a cult cease to be a cult and be called a new religion? Mormonism is now over a century old and, unlike Jehovah's Witnesses, has entered the mainstream of American life. While there are still many fundamentalists who regard any deviation of a movement from biblical teaching as cultic, there does seem to be a point in time when such movements pass from cult to church, and I would suggest that Mormonism has reached that point in time. Having said this, we intend to show that from the Christian perspective it is a false church, leading many sincere people astray.

History

Mormons were persecuted in their early days because they proclaimed all other churches as corrupt, apostate, and spurious and that their church, the true church of Jesus Christ, was re-established after 1,700 years at the command of heaven. The Christian Church, they claimed, went into apostasy after the death of the Apostles, and the reestablished Mormon church alone has true apostolic authority. Modern Mormons still hold to those beliefs.

The founder of the Mormon church was Joseph Smith, Jr., who was born in Sharon, Vermont, in 1805. When he was eleven years old, the family moved to Palmyra, near Rochester, New York, where all but Joseph enrolled in the Presbyterian Church. According to his autobiography in *Pearl of Great Price*, he was confused by the claims of various denominations and couldn't decide which one to join. He often hunted buried treasure in the woods around Palmyra, using "peep stones." When he was fourteen, he was praying in the woods when two "Personages" appeared to him, one pointing to the other and saying, "This is my Beloved Son. Hear Him!" This Personage went on to tell Smith that all the churches were an "abomination in His sight" and that people who belonged to them were vile hypocrites. Three years later, in 1823, Smith was awakened one night by an angel sent from God whose name was Moroni. The angel told Smith that hidden in a nearby hill was a book of golden plates, brought by the Savior for the ancient inhabitants of North America. With the book was a breastplate with silver bows in which were stones called Urim and Thummim. (These names first appear in Leviticus and referred to a receptacle used for casting lots to learn the divine will. Smith's usage made them into a pair of "translator" spectacles.) When Smith looked through Urim and Thummin, he would see the translation of the Reformed Egyptian on the golden plates. Smith claims that the next day he found the plates on a hill called Cumorah.

However, Smith was not allowed to take the plates for four years, when he was entrusted with them until an angel was to call for them. In the meantime he eloped with Emma Hale after her father refused permission to marry because of Smith's visionary ideas and the fact that he thought he could support himself by finding buried money with a "peep stone." According to Smith, he thus began the translation that became the *Book of Mormon*, which told how North and South America were peopled by the lost tribes of Israel who came to the New World in ships, forming two nations, Nephites and Lamanites. Christ, after His resurrection, appeared among the Nephites, selected twelve Indians, and formed a church around them. The Lamanites, however, were evil and attacked the Nephites, destroying them in a battle around Palmyra in A.D. 421. Moroni, son of the Nephite leader Mormon, hid the plates which contained the history of his tribe. The Lamanites became the ancestors of today's American Indians.

Smith translated the *Book of Mormon* from behind a blanket, dictating it to Oliver Cowdery, a former schoolteacher. When the work was published, Cowdery, David Whitmer, and Martin Harris gave testimony as an introduction that they had seen the plates. Later the three men left the cult and Cowdery became a Methodist. With Whitmer, he gave out a statement that the Latter-Day Saints were not a true church. Whitmer published a tract labeling Smith "a false prophet." Harris, under pressure, admitted that he had seen the plates "with eyes of faith" under a cloth. He did return to the Mormons before he died. Once the translation was finished an angel, as promised, came and picked up the plates; thus they were lost to both history and proof.

Once *The Book of Mormon* was in print (financed by Harris), Smith and five followers officially organized the Church of Jesus Christ of Latter-Day Saints, later incorporating it under New York law. Within a month the group had grown to forty members, and steady growth has continued from that time. Smith turned his eyes to the west, sending missionaries to the Indians around Kirtland, Ohio, and then going there himself and publishing the second Mormon sacred book, *Doctrine and Covenants*. A new "revelation" came to Smith, telling him Jackson County, Missouri, was where the city of Zion was to be built. The Mormons went there but ran into conflicts with those settled there. The result was so much trouble that the state militia had to be called out, arresting Smith and some other leaders.

The Mormons retreated east to Illinois, and when Smith and his fellow prisoners escaped, they joined the band. Smith selected a site on the Mississippi River, above Quincy, to build his new center, which he called Nauvoo, mistakenly claiming the word was Hebrew for "beautiful place." The Mormons began erecting a new temple. Smith organized the Nauvoo Legion, a small private army, giving himself the title of lieutenant general. An anti-Smith newspaper, *Nauvoo Expositor*, began a series of articles critical of the Mormons. Smith ordered his Legion to attack the paper and destroy its press. When word of the raid reached the governor of Illinois, he ordered Smith arrested. Smith was later released but then was rearrested along with his brother, Hyrum, and both were taken to jail in nearby Carthage. Feelings ran high against the Mormons, caused by their polygamy and the envy of other settlers at their prosperity. Fearing that the Legion would attack the jail and rescue its prophet, a mob stormed the jail on June 27, 1844, shooting Joseph and Hyrum Smith, thus giving the cult martyrs on whom to build.

Brigham Young, president of the twelve apostles, was elected to head the movement. When Illinois ordered the Mormons out of the state, Young decided that they would move west, seeking the promised land. In February of 1846, with snow still on the ground, four hundred wagons began what was to be a historic and epic journey. Ahead lay cold weather, Indian attacks, apostasy, death, and hunger from short rations. On July 24,

1847, the caravan reached the valley of Salt Lake in Utah. Young made the now famous pronouncement "This is the place." Thus Salt Lake City came into being and prosperity started for the hardworking Mormons. When Brigham Young died in 1877, the group had grown to 140,000 Mormons. Polygamy was a bar to Utah's entry into the Union, so in 1890 Young's successor, Wilford Woodruff, claimed to have received a revelation from God that polygamy was no longer to be enjoyed on earth but was reserved for "the celestial kingdom." Another convenient revelation came to President Kimball in 1978 when the Mormons were under attack for racism. While the sect admitted blacks to membership, no blacks were admitted into the Aaronic priesthood to which most males belong. The problem was resolved when the president was given the "revelation" that blacks could be priests.

Authority for Mormons

Mormons have two sources of religious authority: their scriptures and the continuing revelations of their prophet-president. Mormon scriptures are:

The Bible. This book is valid insofar as it is "correctly translated." Joseph Smith attempted a translation, and what he translated is contained in Pearl of Great Price. The Bible is a difficult book to use in arguing with Mormons. Because they believe it was corrupted in transmission and translation, they can deny any text used against them as being false.

The Book of Mormon. The copy I have is 522 pages long and contains 15 books, named after their supposed authors. This is the history of the American Indians who descended from the Jews as gathered by the Nephite chief Mormon, and this book is accepted by Mormons as the word of God. They get around Joseph Smith's lack of linguistic knowledge by affirming it was translated by the power of God. Smith called it "the most correct book on earth and the keystone to our religion." Much has been written exposing the false claims of this book, which reflects numerous passages from the King James Bible (written a millennium later than the supposed plates). However, it is on science and its historicity that the book fails any objective test. Mormon defense of the book is rich in inconsistencies, improbabilities, and absurdities.

Pearl of Great Price. This a collection of shorter works by Smith, including his personal history (quite at variance with known facts), a portion of Smith's Bible translation (into which he introduced whole new elements not found in any biblical manuscript); the *Book of Abraham* (purportedly from an Egyptian papyrus discovered by Smith), which supposedly was written by Abraham and which contains the infamous charges against blacks; and the *Articles of Faith*, the basis for Mormon beliefs.

Doctrines and Covenants. This work, originally published in 1833 and revised in 1835 and again in 1921 (the latter versions dropping some embarrassing teachings), supplements the "perfect" book of Mormon. Besides containing a message from the Apostle John (taken from a parchment Smith "discovered"), it contains what are now key teachings of the church: organizational structure, the Aaronic and Melchezedek priesthood, the ability of members to become gods, baptism of the dead, celestial marriage, preexistence of the soul, and God as an exalted man. It also teaches the plurality of wives.

The final source of authority is in the leadership structure, the members of which can receive continuing revelations from God. However, only the president can receive revelations that bind the church as a whole. The lesser officers receive revelations pertaining to their duties. In *Doctrines and Covenants* the president is referred to as "a seer, a revelator, a translator, a prophet."

Mormon Doctrines

An important point to remember in speaking of Mormons' doctrines is that their doctrines often contradict their own scriptures, including "that most correct of any book on earth," *The Book of Mormon*. These inconsistencies can be demonstrated by any student of the sect and pointed out to Mormon proselytizers. If they have any explanations, they will of necessity be inventive.

The Trinity. Mormons reject the Christian teaching of the Trinity as one God and three distinct Persons. They use the word "Trinity" but mean three separate gods, two with physical bodies and a third a spirit. These gods cooperate with one another but each is free to go his own way. This doctrine was proclaimed on June 16, 1844, by Joseph Smith in his sermon "The Christian Godhead — A Plurality of Gods" (see *Teachings of Prophet Joseph Smith*). In this sermon Smith mocked the Christian belief, which he called "curious" and "strange." Then in typical confusion he stated: "I have always declared God to be a distinct personage, Jesus Christ a separate and distinct personage from God the Father, and that the Holy Ghost was a distinct personage and a Spirit: and these three constitute three distinct personages and three Gods." Yet in his *Book of Mormon* (Alma 11:44) he states that Father, Son, and Spirit are "one Eternal God." Also as an introduction to *The Book of Mormon* (even today) is printed "The Testimony of Three Witnesses" which concludes: "And the honor be to the Father, and to the Son, and to the Holy Ghost, which is one God." Which Smith is to be believed? Moreover, Mormon teaching is that there are many gods. Smith first introduced the idea of a plurality of gods. Brigham Young continued it: "How many Gods there are, I do not know; but there was never a time when there were not Gods and worlds." Young also taught that man can become a god: As man now is, God once was; as God now is, man may be. So be aware when you are talking to a Mormon that you may be using the same word — "Trinity," for example — yet you may well be talking about entirely different things.

God. The Mormon God is a being that is not all perfect. This is because God is in the state of eternal progression, getting better all the time. God started out as a man, but applying himself to the forces around him, he mastered these. "Thus he grew," writes Mormon theologian Milton R. Hunter in his book *The Gospel Through the Ages*, "in experience and continued to grow until He attained the status of Godhood . . . the road that the Eternal Father followed to Godhood was one of living at all times a dynamic, industrious, and completely righteous life. There is no other way to exaltation." Remember the word "exaltation"? If you recall the boy on the plane at the beginning of this section on Mormons, you may remember that he said he was not afraid to die because he knew he would be exalted. At the time I presumed he meant he expected to be saved. It wasn't until I began studying the Mormons that I realized he meant he was going to become a god. This is the goal of every good Mormon. As Brigham Young said, "What God is, man may be." Mormon teaching postulates three main gods who were responsible for populating the earth: Elohim (Father), Jehovah (Jesus), and Michael (Adam), who took on an earthly body and went to the Garden of Eden with one of his wives, Eve. Thus the human race is descended from a god (Brigham Young, *Discourses* 1:50-51).

Jesus Christ. I remember once seeing a young Mormon missionary sitting with an Indian interpreter outside a house in upland Peru. About ten Indians were reclined on the ground before them. The interpreter was holding a chart of pictures and the one showing was a color picture of Jesus in rather heroic pose. I did not hear what was being said, but if the interpreter was telling the Mormon truth about Jesus, he was not telling of the Christ Christians know. To Mormons, the pre-human Jesus was a brother to Lucifer. Jesus was not the Son of the Father, nor conceived by the Holy Spirit, but born of Adam and Mary, or as Young says, "begotten in the flesh by the same character that was in the Garden of Eden." According to Mormon teaching, Jesus was not unique, because any Mormon can become like Him. Jesus was married at Cana (the wedding feast of the Gospels) and took as His wives "Mary, Martha, and the other Mary also." He also left behind children. By Mormon standards, it was necessary for Jesus to be married, because a single person can only rise to the rank of angel, and not God. Finally, in Mormon teaching, Adam takes precedence over Jesus and the atonement of Jesus was limited because certain grievous sins were beyond the salvation He offered (*Doctrines of Salvation*). If all this sounds confused, it is.

The Book of Mormon mixes the story of Jesus with fact and fiction. Joseph Smith never explained how Nephi and his other Indian authors knew so much about Jesus and at the same time so little. The narrative in 3 Nephi, for example, confuses the Last Supper with the miracle of the loaves and fishes. In the Mormon account, Jesus has the multitude sit down while his apostles go to get bread and wine. After they return Jesus blesses the bread and wine, gives them to the apostles to communicate and then pass on to the multitude. When the distribution is over, Jesus tells his disciples to do this "in remembrance of my blood." The Book of Mormon is full of the experience of Jesus in America, much of it paraphrasing the Gospels but always confused.

Doctrine on Man. Before men appeared on earth, they existed as pre-created spirits. As Brigham Young taught, "Our Father in Heaven begat all the spirits that ever were, or ever will be, on this earth." While Christians believe that God made pure creation out of nothing, Mormons believe matter always existed. Even a spirit is matter, *Doctrines and Covenants* teaches, except that the matter is so fine that it can only be seen with very pure eyes.

While *The Book of Mormon* admits Adam and Eve sinned by eating the apple, the fall was a good thing because after it they could have sexual relations and propagate humanity. Adam returned to heaven, where he will reign as Michael, the prince in charge of all the spirits who will inhabit the earth. The Mormon *Articles of Faith* reject the notion of original sin, saying that we are punished for our own sins, not the sin of Adam.

Salvation. Joseph Fielding Smith, tenth president of the Mormon church, declared in his *Doctrine of Salvation*: "No salvation without accepting Joseph Smith," adding that rejecting Smith's testimony was a bar to entering the Kingdom of God. Brigham Young taught the same thing except he included belief in himself as also necessary for salvation. The Mormon notion that salvation relies heavily on good works disturbs many Protestants who depend solely on faith. "How do we work out our salvation?" asks a Mormon publication. "By participating in the activities of the Church which develop in our souls those Christ-like traits that help us to become like him." Thus Mormon salvation is denied to all non-Mormons since they do not believe in Joseph Smith or the Mormon church.

Baptism. Baptism according to the Mormons must be by immersion. In his revision of the Bible, Joseph Smith had Adam baptized by immersion! Baptism does remit sin, provided there is repentance. Infant baptism is rejected, and *Doctrine and Covenants* specifies that children shall be baptized when they reach the age of eight.

Baptism for the Dead. This is distinctive to the Mormon religion. While *The Book of Mormon* stresses the necessity of baptism for salvation, it says nothing about baptism for the dead. This idea came later to Joseph Smith, who claimed Elijah revealed it to him, when he thought about all who had died before they had the opportunity to receive his "restored Gospel." This authority was given Smith when there appeared to him in the Kirtland (Ohio) Temple "Moses, Elias and Elijah" (Smith was evidently unaware that the latter two were one and the same person, Elias being the Greek form for the Hebrew Elijah). Elijah gave Smith "the keys of sealing power, that all the ordinances for the dead might be performed in a valid way." There is no record of any baptisms of the dead in Kirtland, but they began in Nauvoo, were suspended during the trek west, and resumed in the Salt Lake temple. Speaking of baptism for the dead, Smith said, "Those saints who neglect it in behalf of their deceased relatives, do [so] in the peril of their own salvation."

This obsession of Mormons for having their deceased forebears baptized has led the Mormons to collect the largest accumulation of genealogical records in the world. In fact, the Salt Lake City records have become a prime research source for even non-Mormons. The archives are used by Mormons to seek out relatives. Once they have gained the names they go through a temple ceremony in which the relative is baptized, confirmed in the Mormon church, and then elevated (for males) to the Holy Melchizedek Priesthood. (There are two Mormon priesthoods: the Aaronic, open to obedient males from age twelve, and the Melchizedek, open to obedient males age eighteen.) One ex-Mormon told Gordon H. Fraser (for his book *Is Mormonism Christian?*) that he had been baptized over 5,000 times for the dead. Such a stand-in is known as a Savior on Mount Zion, who has rescued his relatives from Spirit Prison to join other Mormons in Paradise.

The Lord's Supper. As noted, Jesus instituted the Sacrament of the Last Supper when he appeared among the Nephites, and *The Book of Mormon* (Moroni, chapters 4-5) gives the mode for administering the bread and wine, as does *Doctrines and Covenants*. However, Mormon practice is to substitute water for wine. This substitution is conveniently explained: Joseph Smith was on his way to buy wine when he met an angel who told him that it didn't make any difference what the saints drank. The Lord's Supper takes place weekly and all those eight years old and over are expected to attend.

The Temple. The heart of Mormon religious life is the temple. The temple, not to be confused with local Mormon chapels or stakes, is the site of secret and esoteric rites which those who pass through pledge never to reveal. Once a temple has been dedicated, non-Mormons may never enter, but only those Mormons who are found worthy and issued a "temple recommend" following interviews with the stake president (parish head) and the ward bishop (diocesan head). These "recommends" are valid for a year, after which the whole process must be repeated. Before a Mormon obtains his or her first "recommend," a course of study must be undertaken for worthiness, i.e., Mormon standards of dedication, loyalty, financial contribution. During this study none of the secret rituals, handclasps, passwords, etc., are revealed; these await his acceptance as an initiate. Ex-Mormons estimate that only about twenty percent of adult Mormons have such "recommends" and only about ten percent attend temple regularly.

Temple Ceremonies. Since relatively few Mormons obtain the "recommends," relatively few have partaken in temple ceremonies, which are mainly the temple ordinances for the living and for the dead, which in part seem to have borrowed heavily from Masonic rituals with which Smith and his early associates were well acquainted. The ordinances for the living include: washing, anointing, clothing in priesthood garments, and the Endowment. Sealings are performed for married couples and for children with parents. Marriages take place for eternity, but an exception can be given for only a temporal marriage. The marriages are performed in Sealing Rooms and there may be as many as twenty such rooms in a temple. Family and friends can attend the weddings if they have "recommends." The husband is given a secret name for his wife, a name she does not know, but one he can use if he chooses to call her to him in the celestial kingdom. The ordinances for the dead, which are the major number of temple ceremonies, involve baptism, admittance to membership in the church, and ordination to the Melchizedek priesthood.

In the Endowment ceremony the initiate is made privy to the Secrets of the Holy Priesthood, which consist of five laws (Obedience, Sacrifice, Gospel, Chastity, and Consecration), four tokens (handclasps and secret names), and four signs (two signs for the Aaronic priesthood and two for the Melchizedek — the signs are gestures indicating various punishments from throat cutting to dismemberment which are now explained as "various ways life can be taken"), and three penalties . Finally the ones receiving Endowments (including all missionaries) are dressed in the Garment of Holy Priesthood (a type of underwear) which must be worn day and night, 365 days a year. Originally, this garment was like a pair of "long johns," but it is now short-sleeved and cut off at the knees. It is removed only for bathing and to be changed, although an exception is made for "public appearance." The garment has certain priesthood markings, like closed buttonholes over each breast, the navel, and right knee. These markings, handclasps, and oaths are similar to those found in the *Ritual of Masonry* which was on sale in New York State during the time when Hyrum Smith belonged to the Ancient York Rite there. Joseph became a Mason in 1842 in Nauvoo and introduced Masonic symbols in the Nauvoo temple he built.

The "patron" also goes through a two-hour ritual known as the Creation Drama. Formerly, this began with a play enacted in four areas as if four acts. The play features Elohim, Jehovah, Michael, Adam, Eve, and Lucifer, who has a Christian minister as a lackey. In one scene the minister delivers a satirical parody of the Nicene Creed. Today it is a film of about ninety minutes that is well made, if somewhat silly. The Endowment ends with the Veil Ceremony during which patrons (initiates) are tested as to the four tokens and their secret names.

Answering Mormon Missionaries

The young men who come to your door are sincere and believe they are doing God's will in trying to convert you. Respect that sincerity. Few missionaries are converts. Most have been born into their faith, and from the time they have been able to think for themselves they have been instructed in Mormon beliefs by their parents, peers, and in their stakes. They would never think of questioning what they have learned. They have also gone through training in how to approach you. Finally, they are not surprised to meet opposition because they know the persecution their forebears endured for their beliefs. They also have been schooled to answer your objections. They should be treated with Christian love and respect.

While the preceding pages have outlined some of the Mormon doctrines and teachings, the treatment does not pretend to be systematic or complete. Mormon doctrine is complex, convoluted, and sometimes contradictory. It is not recommended that "Gentiles" argue doctrine with Mormons unless they are expert in it. The young missionary may present a specific teaching that can be challenged or responded to on occasion, but the danger here is that you will be led into peripheral issues which do not settle anything. Besides, most people will be at a disadvantage, since the Mormon has been prepared in these matters. It is better to go to the heart of the matter, because it is there that Mormonism is at its weakest.

The Achilles' heel of Mormonism is in its foundation, and it is here that the religion can most easily be shown to be illogical and unreasonable. This foundation is based in two sources: Joseph Smith, Jr., and *The Book of Mormon*.

Joseph Smith, Jr.

Although a case can be made that Joseph Smith was a very strange character indeed, part con man and part impractical dreamer, such a defense is *ad hominem* and weak, because even a con man can do something right. However, the Mormons root their faith in Joseph Smith, and a key Mormon teaching, as has been shown, is "No salvation without accepting Joseph Smith." The Mormons consider Smith a prophet on whom "the Church stands or falls" (Joseph Fielding Smith), and thus the fundamental defense is to show that Joseph Smith was a false prophet. This can be readily done from accepted Mormon documents. Robert A. Morey, in his book *How to Answer a Mormon*, prints page after page of Mormon documentation, underlining the inconsistencies. We summarize several of those findings here:

1. Joseph Smith saw the end of the world and the beginning of the millennium as happening in his generation. This idea was not original with Smith but was common with Adventism. Smith frequently made this prophecy, and *Doctrine and Covenants* cites these propecies given by God to Smith, and prefixing some of them with such words as "Verily I say unto you" (God speaking), "Thus sayeth the Lord," and "I am prepared to say by the authority of Jesus Christ" (Smith speaking). In these prophecies Smith declared the hour was nigh when the earth would be burned up (*Doctrine and Covenants* 29); New York, Albany, and Boston were to be left desolate (*D and C*); Smith would be alive for the coming of Christ (*D and C* 112); the beginning of the end of times would take place in South Carolina (*D and C* 131). In 1835 Smith declared that fifty-six years "should wind up the scene" — thus the millennium was due by 1891, although in 1843 he moved it up to 1890. There is no question that Smith was fascinated by the millennium and believed it would happen shortly.

Smith predicted that the ten lost tribes of Israel were living in the Arctic, would reappear, and would bring their bible with them. This was to happen at the building of a temple in Missouri (*Journal of Discourses* 68). One of Smith's sillier prophecies concerned the race of men who inhabited the moon. O.B. Huntington, who was commissioned to preach to the moon people, recalled, "As far back as 1837, I know that he [Smith] said the moon was inhabited by men and women the same as this earth, and that they lived to greater age than we do — that they live generally to near the age of a thousand years. He described the men as averaging six feet in height and dressing quite uniformly in something near the Quaker style."

Despite setbacks in Missouri from persecution, Joseph Smith prophesied that Zion would be built in Jackson County, Missouri, quoting the Lord to that effect (*D and C* 101). The Lord also said that there was no other place appointed. Yet from history we know Zion was not built there but in Salt Lake City. There are similar predictions (*D and C* 124) about Nauvoo which never came to pass. One need only to read carefully *The Book of Mormon* and *Doctrine and Covenants* to see that Joseph Smith had more imagination than accuracy. Proving one prophecy wrong is enough to show that Smith was a false prophet and hence his religion was founded in error.

Warning: Be aware that the missionary at your door will try to defend the legitimacy of Joseph Smith. He has not been trained in this apologetic because the Mormon leadership does not wish its followers to even think of questioning Smith's word, so they stay away from the subject. Thus you can expect some weaknesses in response, which can vary from insisting that Smith never made prophecies to stating that Smith was only giving his personal opinion. We have previously shown that Smith did make prophecies and that he worded them in such a way that they were commands from God, not his own opinion. Also be aware that the young Mormon may try to change the subject or put you on the defensive by challenging something in Chris-

tian scripture. Do not allow him to do this. Simply say, "We
can discuss the Bible later; right now let us stay with Joseph
Smith."

The Book of Mormon

Mormons have never questioned the history, anthropology,
archaeology, or geography of *The Book of Mormon*. They accept its claims as fact, and it is taught as history in their schools
and propagated worldwide by their missionaries. It is difficult
to understand how scholars at such Mormon institutions as
Brigham Young University, whose disciplines include those
mentioned above, can accept these claims with integrity and a
straight face. It is possible that they don't, that they keep quiet
to protect their positions, but either way their integrity can be
questioned. The facts of *The Book of Mormon* make about as
much sense as Smith's Quaker-dressed people on the moon or
the lost tribes in sunny valleys at the North Pole.

According to *The Book of Mormon*, there were two Semite
migrations to America — the first from the Tower of Babel,
somewhere around 2000 B.C., and the second following the fall
of Jerusalem about 600 B.C. — and its story of Lehi traveling
down the Arabian peninsula gives details of distance and geography, as well as the building of his ship, which can be checked.
All are fictional — distances covered on foot that were impossible to cover in the time given, rivers where no rivers existed, trees for shipbuilding in a desert, mountains where there
are no mountains and so on. The fantastic journey through an
Indian Ocean across the Pacific to the shores of Central America is summarized by saying that after many days they reached
the promised land (America). Nephi does get there by using a
compass (unknown in those days) and on landing finds horses
(which had disappeared from the Americas 25,000 years before
and were reintroduced by the Spaniards in the sixteenth century). The descendants of these people fight their battles with

chariots, horses, metal shields, and swords — all anachronisms (the wheel was unknown in pre-Columbian America). The original *Book of Mormon* was written in Reformed Egyptian, whatever that was. Nowhere in the world is there a record of such a language. Since Nephi and Lehi (the leaders of the migration) were Hebrew, why would they write in a nonexistent language and not use the language of the Bible? We have only Joseph Smith's word for all this, and that is no more reliable than his prophecies. (Moroni has an explanation why Hebrew was not used: Hebrew would take up too much room! [Mormon 9:3].) Although the setting for the Book of Mormon is in Central America (using Maya and Aztec civilizations), the last great battle of the tribes takes place around a remote hill in upstate New York, and when it is lost (hundreds of thousands have been killed) Moroni buries his plates right next to where the Smith farm will be.

Where did Smith get the ideas for *The Book of Mormon?* Mostly from his imagination, but he did have help. In reading *The Book of Mormon*, one immediately notes the number of expressions and phrases taken from both the Old and New Testaments (King James Version) which no Central American Indian would know or think of writing in King James idiom; the similarities are too frequent and great to be coincidental. Mormon critics also claim that Smith borrowed from other books that were available in his time: a historical novel by the Rev. Solomon Spalding about the origins of the American Indians; *View of the Hebrews* by Ethan Smith (published in Poultney, Vermont, where Oliver Cowdrey lived); and *The Wonders of Nature* by Josiah Priest (Albany, N. Y., 1825).

Mormons have gone to great lengths to defend the integrity of *The Book of Mormon*, one of them being that the Smithsonian Institution in Washington had approved its history and uses it as a guide for research. A paper produced by Mormons boasted that the Smithsonian quotes the book "as an authority" and that it "is recognized by all advanced students in the field."

When these claims came to the attention of the Institute, a statement was issued that said: "The Smithsonian Institution has never officially recognized *The Book of Mormon* as a record of value on scientific matters, and the *Book* has never been used as a guide or source of information for discovering ruined cities."

Mormon Structures. The Mormons have a complex hierarchy. At the head is the successor of Joseph Smith, the President, who is described as "a seer, a revelator, a translator, and a prophet." While any Mormon can be given a revelation from God, only the President can receive one which binds the whole LDS Church. The President with two Counselors make up the First Presidency. Next comes the Council of the Twelve Apostles and then the Presidency of the First Quorum of the Seventy (seven presidents and members of the quorum). There is a Presiding Bishopric (three members) and a Presiding Patriarch who can bless and curse, bind and loose. These upper levels are paid ministries. Below are national quorums, divided into wards presided over by bishops, and then parishes called stakes, governed by a President. Neither ward leader nor stake leader are paid positions.

Buildings. When a friend was reading this section in manuscript, he remarked that I made a mistake when I wrote about restrictions on entering Mormon temples. He said he had seen crowds in the temple on television and that he was sure tourists were permitted inside. I had to tell him he was wrong. He was talking about tabernacles, not temples.

The temple is the center of Mormon religious life where their strange rites take place. Temples in Salt Lake City, Los Angeles, and Washington rise above the surrounding skyline topped by a golden angel, Moroni, blowing his trumpet — a familiar sight to passersby. There are other temples in Canada, Europe, and elsewhere. Tabernacles are fewer, and the best known is in Salt Lake City, made familiar to television viewers with its Mormon Tabernacle Choir. It serves as an auditorium for assemblages of the church and can be entered by anyone. The buildings in a local area are called chapels, and these serve not only for worship but for social occasions and general usage. The Mormons also erect other buildings to serve the business activities of the church and as warehouses where people tithe for the expected rainy day.

Mormon Schisms. Kate Carter in *Our Pioneer Heritage* says that sixty sects have split from the Mormon Church, of which about twenty are still in existence. These sects arose from private revelations, supposedly given to their founders, that they were to succeed Joseph Smith or that something the parent church was doing was wrong.

The largest of these schismatic churches is the Reorganized Church of Jesus Christ of Latter-Day Saints, which has its headquarters in Independence, Missouri, and numbers some 300,000 members. This church is sometimes called the Josephites after its first leader, Joseph Smith III, son of the original prophet, and since its founding has always had a descendant of the prophet as its head. Its founding Mormons broke away from Brigham Young and claimed to be the true successors of Joseph Smith. They were made up of dissidents who didn't like the polygamy that was beginning to grow within Mormonism and objected to political actions of the prophet. It was this group that began an opposition newspaper which Joseph Smith ordered destroyed, a command that led to his murder. This group rejects parts of *Doctrine and Covenants*, and all of *Pearl of Great Price*. It accepts *The Book of Mormon* as the word of God and the Bible as "containing" the word of God when it agrees with Joseph Smith's translation. It rejects baptism of the dead, the Adam-god concept, and temple worship.

Other sects with relatively few followers include the Strangites, which centered in Wisconsin and attracted the brother of Joseph Smith; the Bickertonites of Kansas; the Fettingites, which began in Michigan; and the Hendrickites, which managed to gain possession of the piece of ground Smith had set aside in Independence for his temple and who hold the land to this day despite suits and pressures to buy from the mother church. There are also polygamous cults in Utah which occasionally make headlines around the country because of some violence but which tend to fade away with the death of their leaders. These breakaway churches are not as aggressive as the Utah mother church, although the Reorganized branch does have missionaries.

Remember These Points

1. Remember to treat the Mormon missionary with Christian love and not to be antagonistic. He believes in what he is saying, so recognize his sincerity and do not ridicule beliefs that seem silly to you.

2. Remember that in talking about God, Jesus, the Trinity, etc., he is talking about something different from what you understand by such words. Ask what is meant by such words. Even the word "Christian" needs to be defined, since he considers himself a Christian, which he is not in the traditional and accepted sense.

3. Unlike the Jehovah's Witness, the Mormon will not attack your Faith as much as he will try to persuade you to his.

4. As we have pointed out, the Mormon faith is so complex that you will become lost and confused if you try to argue it dogma by dogma. This takes expertise.

5. Also as noted, the weakest points in Mormonism are the prophecies of Joseph Smith and the text of *The Book of Mormon*. If you can master the critique of these you can plant doubts in the Mormon mind, although if the Mormon thinks his faith is being undermined, he may quickly retreat.

6. Invite your Mormon visitors to come back and learn more about Christianity from you.

8

The Churches of Christ

HE WAS A young pitcher who dreamed of a career in the big leagues. For the time being he had to endure the purgatory of the bush leagues, traveling from town to town by bus, bored with take-out food, and desperately lonely for his distant family. He had been raised a Catholic, but away from home he began missing his Sunday obligation, excusing himself because of travel or getting ready for a Sunday afternoon game.

In time he was assigned to a team in a southern city. He noticed a girl, sometimes alone, sometimes with another girl, frequently in the stands at his home field. One day before a game he stopped to talk to her; then one thing led to another, and before long they were dating. He admired the girl, whom he found sincerely committed to Christianity, and when she invited him to go to church with her he accepted. It was not like a church that he was used to, but its emphasis on fundamental Christianity, its *a capella* singing, the friendliness of its members, all proved attractive.

When his team was at home he attended church regularly with the girl, whom he was now dating. She suggested that he become a member, and he agreed. An elder told him he would have to be baptized, and when he explained that he had already been baptized he was told that infant baptism and non-immersion baptism were unscriptural and invalid. So he was immersed and in time married the young lady who had won him to her church. When his mother came to town for the wedding, upset over his apostasy, and asked me to talk with him, I did. He explained that he now only believed what was present in the Scriptures, that denominationalism was wrong, that he felt very close to Jesus, that the main-line churches had become lost in their structures, and that he was very content with his New Testament church and becoming a Christian. He told me that there were a number of former Catholics in his church and that they were all very happy there. I realized that there was little I could do at the moment and invited him back at any time. His new church had a firm hold upon him, and I never saw him again.

I first became aware of his new church some years earlier. There was a small white clapboard building along the highway leading into a town where I then lived that one day put up a roadside sign which simply said:

Church of Christ
Founded 33 A.D.

It was a claim that irritated some of the Protestant pastors in town, and after a while the sign disappeared. I don't know whether it was voluntarily taken down or stolen but in time a new one went up that simply said: "Church of Christ."

What the local pastors were objecting to was the claim that this Church of Christ went back to the time of Jesus, when in fact it arose out of the Campbellite movement early in the last century. That movement was named after Thomas and Alexander Campbell, father and son. Thomas Campbell came to this country from Ireland and became minister to a Presbyterian church southwest of Pittsburgh, Pennsylvania. He shocked his small congregation with unorthodox ideas, with the result that he was forced to resign his pulpit in 1809 and with a few followers began a nondenominational group called the Christian Association. Thomas was joined by his son Alexander, who was gaining a reputation as a preacher.

The motto of the new group was: "Where the Scriptures speak, we speak; where the Scriptures are silent, we are silent." The Campbells called their movement a New Testament restoration, used the Lord's Supper, and insisted on baptism by immersion. For a time they affiliated with the Baptists, and Alexander edited the *Christian Baptist*, which he used to denounce his pet aversions, such as Catholics and creeds, clergy and choirs, Calvinists and church organizations. In time the Campbells came to the conclusion that the Baptists were just another creed, so they departed with their followers, calling themselves Disciples of Christ.

By the time of the Civil War the Disciples claimed a quarter of a million followers. Thomas Campbell had died in 1854, but Alexander had taken leadership of the movement years earlier. He wrote reams of copy and traveled widely, lecturing and preaching to persuade others to his ideas of a scriptural simplicity in organization and doctrine. But as the Disciples of Christ grew, the church became more structured and a conservative faction developed that was resistant to changes. Thus the Disciples became known for a mixed membership of conservatives and progressives, with the latter being in control. When in 1906 the progressive pastors began allowing instrumental music at church services, it was too much for the conservatives. They broke away and organized the Churches of Christ.

Today the Churches of Christ form one of the largest Christian denominations, claiming a membership of 2.5 million, mainly in the south and west of the United States. The member churches are highly individualistic, with each congregation being autonomous. Congregations are small, the group boasting some 20,000 separate churches. For example, in Nashville, Tennessee, the group claims 40,000 members in 135 congregations — an average of slightly less than 300 members per congregation. The Churches of Christ also claim representation in about 110 countries. It is very difficult to check these figures out.

The problem in writing about the Churches of Christ is that it is very difficult to generalize. Each congregation is self-ruled and independent of every other congregation. Hence, each congregation takes on the characteristics of its membership and leadership, which can vary considerably from group to group. The Churches of Christ boast that they "have none of the trappings of modern-day organizational bureaucracy. There are no governing boards — neither district, regional, national or international — no earthly headquarters and no man-designed organization." There are no conventions, no annual meetings, no official publications.

The Churches of Christ boast that they are not a denomination. Denominations, they say, are man-made creeds. Their only creed is the New Testament, and despite their Campbellite and Disciples heritage they believe they are the church Jesus established. I suppose that was the reason for the "Founded 33 A.D." sign I saw. They call themselves "people of a restoration spirit," who are restoring the first-century New Testament church in our times. Anti-Catholic, they forget that the canonicity of their New Testament was selected by the Catholic Church, quite a few years after the first century. Nevertheless, they take the New Testament as God's blueprint and the only way to return to the original church: "If it isn't in the New Testament, then it should not be done." This eliminates all other denominations and marks them as false because they have added structures and developed teachings beyond the New Testament. They are willing to accept the traditions of apostolic times but reject the traditions of those who knew the Apostles.

Each congregation is governed by a plurality of elders selected from among the members, saying they base this office on 1 Timothy 3 and Titus 1. But Paul is not talking about elders in these sections. In 1 Timothy he is speaking of bishops

and deacons, and in Titus of presbyters or priests, indicating
that the early Church was already being structured with a hierarchy. So in their leaders they are already departing from the
New Testament pattern. Besides elders, they also have deacons,
and in this they do follow the letter to Timothy.

The religious service composes a fivefold pattern: singing,
praying, preaching, giving, and eating the Lord's Supper. They
make a big point of their *a cappella* singing. They note that
there are eight verses in the New Testament that mention singing — one in the Gospel of Matthew, one in Acts, and six in
various Pauline letters — and since none of these verses mention
any musical instruments, they are banned. In this they are in
the pattern of John Calvin and John Wesley. They fail to see
that their claim is really a *non sequitur* — simply because musical instruments are not mentioned, this does not mean they were
not used. Preaching is fundamentalist, praying is Protestant,
and giving follows a universal custom, although some of the requests for funds are for non-New Testament purposes. Their
Lord's Supper is symbolic, and they do not associate it with
John 6:52-56, where Jesus speaks of the reality of the Eucharist. Unlike many Protestant churches which have occasional
celebrations of the Lord's Supper, their observance is weekly.

They do not practice infant baptism because baptism is only
for sinners and no infants were baptized in the New Testament.
"An infant," says one of their publications, "has no sin to re-
pent of, and cannot qualify as a believer." Thus they negate
original sin and develop another *non sequitur*. While there is no
mention of the baptism of an infant in the New Testament, that
is not to say that the family of Cornelius, who was baptized with
his family by Peter, or that of the jailer, who was baptized with
"his whole family" by Paul, did not contain children. They admit that baptism is necessary for salvation and to enter the kingdom, thus ruling both out for children who die before baptism.
The only form of baptism they admit is by immersion.

Earlier we mentioned the autonomy of the congregation and

also that some of their collections were for non-New Testament purposes. They do support such things as collective broadcasting, television, and periodicals, none of which are mentioned in the New Testament. The congregations contribute to the annual budget of the Church of Christ in Abilene, Texas, which carries on a national radio and television apostolate. Combined funds also purchase newspaper advertising, offering correspondence courses in their teachings. They join together for supporting missionaries, and combined funds are also used to underwrite a half-dozen colleges — Pepperdine and Abilene Christian being the better known. While these colleges claim to be nondenominational, they are supported by church money, their trustees must be members of the church, and their chapel services and religious instruction are according to church teaching.

Unlike the Disciples of Christ, which have a strong ecumenical tradition, the Churches of Christ tend to be exclusive, rejecting Catholic and Protestant churches as inventions of men. They are particularly opposed to the Pentecostal churches and the pentecostal movement. While pentecostal gifts are mentioned in the New Testament, they teach that they ended with the deaths of the Apostles. They regard those who speak in tongues, faith healers, prophets, etc., to be dupes of Satan. Some years ago when Pat Boone, a Church of Christ member, mentioned in an interview that he believed in speaking in tongues, both he and his wife were disfellowshipped from the Church of Christ.

We have gone into the Churches of Christ at some length because they are making inroads among Catholics and mainline Protestants who may be unsatisfied with their own church structures or seeking an emotional fellowship not found in the main-line churches. Simplicity is easily understood and often attractive when the historical development of one's own faith is not known. While these churches are highly evangelistic, they do not possess the aggressiveness of the Mormons and Witnesses. Instead of knocking at your door, members are more likely to slip literature under your door, although some zealous members are known to go door to door. On the whole, however, they depend on advertising and broadcasting to make themselves known. Members are, however, encouraged to bring friends to their Sunday gatherings and Bible studies, and it is often such a simple invitation that leads away a member of another church.

9

Unity Church

A COLUMN I write draws a great deal of reader mail, and quite frequently I get letters asking about a publication called *Daily Word* that the writers are receiving as a gift from a friend. Evidently, the letter writers have had their suspicions or curiosity raised by this attractive little magazine with its four-color art, its spiritual thoughts, and its capability to be slipped in purse or pocket for occasional reading. When I publish a reply that *Daily Word* is the product of a cult and they shouldn't be reading it, there is a deluge of protests from readers who rise to its defense and tell me that they get great spiritual comfort from it.

Daily Word, along with *Unity, Weekly Unity,* and *Wee Wisdom* are published by the Unity Church, which prefers the name Unity School of Christianity but is a church nonetheless, with an ordained ministry and centers in cities and towns throughout the United States. It also claims to be nondenominational but is a direct descendant of Christian Science and New Thought. It adopted the name "Unity" in 1891, but it had been founded earlier by Charles and Myrtle Fillmore as a faith-healing cult.

New Thought, which emphasizes "the creative power of constructive thinking," grew out of New England Transcendentalism. It was the combined brainchild of "Dr." Phineas P.

Quimby, a faith healer, and Warren Felt Evans, a Sweden-borgian minister, who was the litterateur for Quimby's ideas. Mary Baker Eddy, the founder of Christian Science, was both a patient and a student of Quimby, and it was his ideas that she used to develop her own cult. Originally concerned with healing disease, the movement developed an optimistic philosophy of conduct based on the constructive power of the mind, a system which embodies ideas borrowed from Christianity as well as pantheistic, spiritualistic, cabalistic, and theosophical thought.

Charles and Myrtle Fillmore had studied Quimby's and Eddy's teachings and found their ideas attractive. Mrs. Fillmore, who had been sickly but recovered, attributed her cure to the power of her mind. "I am a child of God and therefore I do not inherit sickness," she wrote. By 1891 the Fillmores had formulated their philosophy, borrowing elements from New Thought and Christian Science but making their own applications. Unlike Christian Science, they admitted illness was a reality but one that could be overcome by positive thinking. They called their new movement Unity and began to propagate it. From the beginning the Fillmores recognized the power of direct mail, and they built up extensive mailing lists with which they could sell their publications and propagate their cause. When the Fillmores died, their sons carried on the work.

Unity professes faith in "Jesus Christ preaching." It accepts the Bible but only allegorically and not literally. It teaches that revelation was not final with the Apostles but is an ongoing, continuous process. The movement believes that eventually all will be saved, passing through various reincarnations until the proper Christian consciousness is developed and ultimate Unity is reached. The movement claims to be nondenominational and allows adherents to remain in their original churches, but the expectation is that those who are in contact with the movement will be drawn to Unity centers for their spiritual needs and thus become total adherents.

Unity headquarters can be found on a 1,300-acre former

farm in Lee's Summit, a suburb of Kansas City, Missouri. Here one finds the cult's administration building, printing plant, seminary, audiovisual production plant, motel, and recreation area. Besides the extensive printing and mailing operations, Lee's Summit is also the base for Silent Unity, a twenty-four-hour prayer service that responds to telephone and written appeals. Although there is no charge for this service, "love offerings" are encouraged. It is said that over a million requests are handled each year. Unity ministers, who are trained in counseling, are educated here and then assigned to the group's churches or centers around the country, often charged with starting new ones.

Unity has had considerable success in gaining support of people who have no idea of the cult's teaching. This is largely because of *Daily Word*, which is not as doctrinal as some other Unity publications, which gives more the impression of bland do-goodism, but which nonetheless reflects the basic philosophy of the cult. Most of the audience for *Daily Word* are women, beyond the yuppie years, who find there the solace and inspiration they so often need. It is not a critical audience, and it remains unaware of the religious bias behind the publication. Without their knowing it, their Catholic or Protestant faiths are undermined. A few Catholic and Protestant publications have tried to imitate *Daily Word*, but none has successfully caught its formula (although *My Daily Visitor*, a pocket-size bimonthly with meditations geared to the liturgical year [Our Sunday Visitor, Inc., Huntington, Ind.] offers much more substantial fare).

Unity may not be a stranger at your door but can well be a stranger in your mailbox, ultimately the more dangerous to faith because you bring it into your home.

10

The Televangelists

WHILE THE strangers who come to your door must have an invitation to enter, the televangelists are already there, preaching their messages and seeking your support. You need but turn on your radio or television and twist your dial and you will find them. Some of them are nondenominational, like Southern Baptist-trained Billy Graham, preaching a fundamental biblical doctrine that is nonsectarian and of wide appeal. Some are sectarian, preaching the faith of their church mainly to coreligionists, and interpret their work as an outreach of a local ministry. Others are "anti" preachers, spewing venom against Pentecostals, Catholics, and even main-line Protestant churches. Still others have cultic aspects (centering their programs on a charismatic personality), seek a national audience, and are as much fund-raisers as preachers. It is some of the latter that one must be careful of, as your donations can be used for anything from personal aggrandizement — multiple homes, airplanes, and high living — to missions that undermine the faith of fellow believers.

Many people who would never think of walking off the street into a church of a different creed will bring a preacher of that faith into their homes electronically, will give him an uncritical hearing, and will often be moved to lend their financial support without fully realizing to what they are contributing.

One of the dangers of the electronic church is that it often gives a sense of personal power to its practitioners, and very often that power corrupts. Some, again like Billy Graham, keep the proper perspective and attribute their success to God. Others, however, take it personally, and most of us are aware of the fall of Jim Bakker and Jimmy Swaggart. The results appear in headlines, such as the one in the *Wall Street Journal*:

The Electronic Church
Aim: 'Hearts and Pocketbooks'

We should also be aware that, for many, worship at home has replaced the local church, much to the detriment of organized religion. It is what the Lutheran theologian Martin Marty calls "the invisible religion."

Televangelism began almost at the outset of radio. A. F. Harlow, in *Old Wires and New Waves* (Ayer Co. Pubs., Salem, N. H.), tells how Reginald Fessenden broadcast to ships at sea from Massachusetts on Christmas Eve of 1906: "Early that evening wireless operators on ships within a radius of several hundred miles sprang to attention as they caught the call 'CQ, CQ' in the Morse code. Was it a ship in distress? They listened eagerly, and to their amazement heard a voice coming from their instruments — someone speaking! Then a woman's voice rose in song. It was uncanny! Many of them called to their officers to come and listen; soon the wireless rooms were crowded." Harlow goes on to describe this first radio broadcast in history: Fessenden playing "O Holy Night" on the violin, then reading the Nativity Gospel from Luke, and concluding with a phonograph recording of Handel's "Largo" from *Serse*. Commercial radio programming began in 1920 at KDKA in Pittsburgh, and within two months there was a regular religious broadcast.

Protestants were quick to realize the potential of the new medium. The Gospel Tabernacle of Chicago took to the airwaves over WBBM, and thousands crowded the Tabernacle each week to see the preacher they had heard on radio. R. R. Brown of the Christian and Missionary Alliance is said to have formed the first radio congregation over WOW in Omaha in 1923. Then as now, it was not the main-line churches that were using the new medium but individuals and small separate groups. The religious broadcasters saw in radio a way of fulfilling the command of Christ to "preach to all nations," and they recognized that through the medium they could reach people otherwise unavailable. As radio grew, the Federal Communications Commission took charge and instituted a rule that each station had to devote a percentage of time to public service; quickly religious groups applied for a share of this time, and such programs as "The Catholic Hour," "National Radio Pulpit," and "Lutheran Hour" developed. But what the main-line churches did not learn, and haven't learned to this day, but what the individual religious entrepreneurs knew, is that if you want to pick your time and develop your audience, you must pay for the time.

The leading electronic evangelists today all pay their own way; all are individual efforts, and each is successful, more so than all the main-line churches combined. An annual survey revealed that in an average week almost fifty percent of the American population turned on at least one electronic religious program while only forty percent attended a church service. Moreover, the influence of these apostolates extends far beyond the borders of the United States. Radio and television programs operated by born-again American Christian groups have the capability of beaming the Gospel via satellite to ninety percent of the world's population, according to Ben Armstrong of National Religious Broadcasters. While radio is still used extensively, particularly outside the United States, it is television that has created a host of new religious stars: among them, Jimmy Swaggart, James Kennedy, Kenneth Copeland, John Ankerberg, Ernest Angley, James Robison, Pat Robertson,

Jerry Falwell, Robert Schuller, Richard De Haan, and Oral Roberts.

In addition to these national luminaries, there are scores and scores of local preachers, each with his or her own following. Many of the national programs began locally and grew. Many a preacher has taken to the airwaves to combat his own diminishing church attendance, beginning first on radio where costs are relatively low and then expanding to television. Ben Armstrong, in his book *The Electric Church*, gives case studies. He tells of one Presbyterian church in a city of a quarter of a million people. A live telecast was begun of the Sunday morning service which raised church attendance to over three thousand, with an average TV audience of forty-five thousand viewers.

What the electronic media can do for the individual parish, it can also do for the mother church. The Assemblies of God is a good example. This church, which numbered about 300,000 members in 1950, has today grown to over two million in the United States and fourteen million overseas (nine million in Brazil), largely through missionary effort supported by its electronic apostolate to which the group's star performer, Jimmy Swaggart, contributed millions each year before he was expelled. Jim Bakker, another defrocked Assemblies of God preacher, also aided in its growth.

The Assemblies of God grew out of disaffected Methodists who gravitated toward the Pentecostal and Holiness movements that gained popularity after the Civil War, developing such denominations as the Church of the Nazarene and the Assemblies of God. This latter church was organized in Hot Springs, Arkansas, in 1914 and later moved its headquarters to Springfield, Missouri. Although each congregation is largely self-governing, Springfield is home of the General Council and thirteen executives, including a General Superintendent, who decide policy, regulate the clergy, and direct its 11,000 congregations in the United States, 30,000 ministers (ten percent women), and over a thousand missionaries abroad. The church conducts a number of colleges with its main training college, Central Bible College, being in Springfield, where an extensive printing plant turns out tons of religious literature.

Most all these electronic preachers offer a highly personal, emotional brand of religion, and insist on the Bible as being without error and the basic source of faith. Those from the Baptist tradition are strict fundamentalists, while those from Pentecostal backgrounds offer a highly-charged emotional, yet puritanical, experience, including Baptism of the Spirit, speaking in tongues, and faith healing. It is this appeal to emotions that has attracted huge audiences in Latin America but which, according to some observers, may be the Achilles' heel of the movement, since a peak in emotions cannot be sustained over a long period. There is another inborn danger. As these movements grow and prosper, their initiators gain great wealth and power, both of which can corrupt. Some attribute this very fact as the reason of the fall from grace of Jimmy Swaggart and Jim and Tammy Bakker. The danger is always there.

Viewers of some of these television ministries about to be discussed should be aware of the dangers and emotionalism and should have some idea of how donations are accounted for (not what the preacher says) before contributing. Some of these ministers have all the charms of a snake-oil salesman.

Jimmy Swaggart

Of all the religious TV pitchmen, none can match the histrionics of Jimmy Swaggart. Some critics have called him more entertainer than revivalist. Certainly, he has taken hints from his cousins, rockabilly musician Jerry Lee Lewis and country-western promoter Mickey Gilley. He parades back and forth across the stage like an angry lion, one hand raised with an open Bible, the other with his wireless microphone, sweat drenching his face, his collar and tie partly open so that his shirt is not buttoned at the neck. His voice goes from shouting to whispers, and at any given moment he can break out in tears; no other evangelist can cry as well, except for his son, Donny, who is being groomed as heir.

Swaggart's message is basic but impassioned fundamentalist. Ordained in the Assemblies of God Church but now independent, he preaches the pentecostalism of that sect. Although he claims that he has been speaking in tongues since the age of nine, he refrains from this display on stage. To hear him speak one would conclude that the Second Coming is right at hand. His most scathing remarks are aimed at the main-line churches that he claims have deserted Christ. He has no use for Catholics, damning both Pope John Paul II and Mother Teresa to hell because they have not been born again and "come out of that church" which has traditions that are anti-God. He is particularly bitter about the celibacy imposed on priests, saying, "Forbidding to marry has caused untold immorality in the Catholic Church. Innumerable sordid, tragic, and sometimes vile scandals have resulted from this perverted insistence on ostensible celibacy." That was said before his own adulterous infidelity and fall from grace.

Although his father was a Louisiana moonshiner, Swaggart, whose formal education ended before he completed high school, was brought up in tub-thumping backwoods faith that is so prevalent in the South. While his cousins turned to music to escape their environment, Swaggart found his escape in religion. He was just another itinerant preacher until he discovered radio and television and developed them into the Jimmy Swaggart Evangelistic Association, a $150-million-a-year empire that enjoys a weekly audience of over two million Americans and reaches into foreign countries with emphasis on Latin America. All of this is directed from His World Faith Center in Baton Rouge, Louisiana. From this base he makes his broadcasts, directs his radio station, and records his telecasts, which he distributes through syndication to over 200 stations and various cable systems. Swaggart's main strength is in the South where half his audience lives; another quarter is in the Midwest, and the remaining quarter equally divided between East and West. Unlike most ministries, which largely attract women, Swaggart appeals equally to men and women.

To support this enterprise and its many employees, Swaggart has had to extend himself well beyond preaching into fundraising. His television appeals for money are not as heavily laden as, say, those of Jerry Falwell, since he relies on direct mail and his monthly magazine, *The Evangelist*, which he also uses to attack his "enemies." It was in the magazine that he savaged Catholics, whom he called "poor, pitiful individuals who think they have enriched themselves spiritually by kissing the pope's ring." He also railed in the magazine against such Catholic practices as the Eucharist, the Sacrament of Reconciliation, the priesthood, and the papacy, all of which are "un-Christian." *The Evangelist*, which has a circulation approaching a million, is about fifty percent hard-sell in-house advertising.

Swaggart, who entertains as much as he preaches, takes to the piano each program and renders gospel music with a beat. *The Evangelist* offers his recordings in records, tapes, and cassettes. He also offers recordings of his sermons. *The Evangelist* also sells such items as Bibles, Christmas cards, calendars, hymn books, and various "Jesus Saves" sundries. The magazine is used to promote travel tours. Jimmy and his wife, Frances, led one tour to the Holy Land and another to Hawaii. Some items have been offered for "donations" and thus became tax-deductible. Few tricks are missed in order to bring in the multi-millions needed to keep the operation afloat.

Disciplined for sexual misconduct by local and national Assemblies of God leadership, Swaggart accepted only the former body's more lenient suspension and continues his ministry separated from the parent church. His fall caused financial reverses, but now, back on the air, he is expected slowly to recoup.

Jerry Falwell

Jerry Falwell, the founder of the Old Time Gospel Hour, is a victim of his own success. About half of his television hour each week must be spent in raising funds to support the ministry he has created instead of devoting itself to the word of God. Falwell, who gives off an affable, avuncular presence, is so well respected in the electronic religious community that in 1987 he was selected to hold together Jim Bakker's PTL ministry when that effort fell on hard times after its founder was defrocked by the Assemblies of God for sexual conduct unbecoming a minister. But the PTL Club and its religious theme park were in such financial shambles that Falwell quickly departed lest his own ministry suffer.

Jerry Falwell was born in Lynchburg, Virginia, and has spent his whole life there, except for a few years in the Midwest at Baptist Bible College. He frequently tells his story on television and has written an autobiography which he offers to donors as a premium. His father, Carey, was a local businessman who had a predilection for the bottle and no time for religion and whose drinking led to his death at age fifty-five. His mother, Helen, was a religious woman who had little success getting Jerry and his twin brother to church on Sundays and made up for it by blaring Charles Fuller's Old Fashioned Revival Hour on the radio. Jerry was a sophomore in Lynchburg College studying engineering when, at the age of eighteen, he had a conversion experience. He began attending Park Avenue Baptist Church and there met Macel Pate, who was to become his wife. He left college for the seminary.

In 1956, as a newly ordained Baptist minister, Jerry Falwell returned to Lynchburg to begin what was to become the Thomas Road Baptist Church, the second-largest Baptist parish in the nation. (The largest is W. A. Criswell's First Baptist Church of Dallas, Texas, also a ministry built out of a radio apostolate. Criswell was once introduced by Falwell as "the

Protestant Pope of this generation.") Falwell began his church with thirty-five members in an abandoned soft-drink bottling plant. Within a week he had a daily radio program and six months later was on local television with his new parish growing by leaps and bounds, thanks both to his broadcasting and a bus ministry. Success breeds new ambition, and by 1970 Thomas Road Baptist Church moved into its third home, the present Early-American auditorium, completely equipped for television. The following year he founded Liberty Baptist College, a training seminary whose graduates are sent about the country to establish new Baptist parishes in the Falwellian theological mold. In 1973 Liberty University came into existence, a coed school that aims to give its students a sense of evangelical mission. This was followed by Liberty Missionary Society, dedicated to foreign missions, and a home for pregnant girls where they can have their babies and not abort them.

All of this expansion costs far more than the local parish can supply, hence the hard sell each Sunday on the Old Time Gospel Hour. While Falwell himself has claimed as high as twenty-five million viewers, and his associates up to fifty million, the Religious Broadcasters Association estimates three million and impartial sources give two million. Even at the last figure, it is a huge weekly audience, and the banks of phones the ministry maintains proves that it is a responsive audience. Falwell does not sell goods over TV but promises premiums for donations. These premiums have included Bibles printed for the ministry by Thomas Nelson, tapes of the Bible and Falwell talks, his autobiography, and Faith Partner pins. His aim is to convert donors into sponsors, people who pledge so much each month. At times the appeals can become frantic hard sells, as when donations fell off at the time of the Bakker scandal and he owed money to TV stations for time bought. Direct-mail appeals are also made.

Unlike Jimmy Swaggart, Falwell is not a hell-and-brimstone preacher. He presents a sedate worship service with a few hymns and his sermon. He projects an image of a careful, restrained preacher, wholly convinced of the validity of his Baptist message. He prefers to be called fundamentalist rather than Baptist, and his church is not affiliated with the Southern Baptist Convention. A book on the electronic apostolate, *Prime Time Preachers*, sums Falwell up this way: " 'The Old Time Gospel Hour' is a bastion of frontier fundamentalism moved uptown." He does not make personal attacks on others and has even invited Senator Ted Kennedy, with whom he strongly disagrees, to speak at his Lynchburg center. His message is the Bible as interpreted by Falwell, and he lets all know that he is opposed to abortion, smut, Women's Liberation, and sex education in schools. He is a persuasive speaker, appealing more to the intellect than the emotions in his low-key way, and for that reason probably will have a longer and more effective life than his more flamboyant counterparts.

In 1980 Falwell moved strongly into politics with his Moral Majority and put the fear of something, if not God, into the liberal left; however, he kept this apart from his Thomas Road ministry and has since ceased to take an active role. He makes a good salary but has never been accused of using his ministry for high living and was a charter member of the Evangelical Council for Financial Accountability, which the other religious media stars studiously shunned.

Even among Southern Baptists, his appeal is to the right wing of the Church. His preaching reflects the fact that he accepts the Bible literally and as his only guide. Every word in it is the infallible word of God, not subject to interpretation but to be accepted as written. While he doesn't openly condemn other Christian groups, he lets it be known that man-made rules are to be rejected. He is a long way from Catholic teaching, yet many Catholics send support because they like what he says about the Bible and are moved by his appeals, not realizing that they are also supporting missions that will proselytize against their Church both in the United States and in Latin America.

Oral Roberts

Along with Jerry Falwell, Oral Roberts is one of the pioneering TV evangelists. Where Falwell always appears to be smiling, Roberts surrounds himself in lugubriousness and solemnity. Where Falwell's energy gives the impression that he is in the prime of his ministry, Roberts appears as one winding down and preparing his second son, Richard, to take over the Oral Roberts Evangelistic Association. Like other evangelists, he has built himself an empire — Oral Roberts University, City of Faith Medical Center — and is hard put to raise funds to keep the empire afloat. Unlike most of the other TV luminaries, Roberts paid hard dues to get to the top.

Granville Oral Roberts was born in rural Oklahoma, the son of an impoverished Pentecostal Holiness preacher. In his autobiography, *The Call*, he recounts the hardships of his early life which led him to run away and fend for himself. Stricken by tuberculosis, he finally returned home, where he was "touched by the hand of God" and cured of his sickness. In 1935 he was commissioned a Pentecostal Holiness preacher like his father and became a pastor in Enid, Oklahoma, a bustling oil town. He believed, however, that his mission was to the many and not the few. "God has called me to bring healing to this generation," he said at one time, and the way he decided this could be done was through tent revival meetings. As Roberts traveled from town to town his reputation grew, and big crowds turned out for his revivals, each of which featured healing sessions. He had no theological education but preached his version of the Bible in what was called the "world's largest Gospel tent."

While continuing his tent meetings of healing and revival, Roberts began a radio program to reach a wider audience. About 1953 he met with Rex Humbard, another evangelist, who told him he ought to get into the developing medium of television. The following year he began a television program, filming his sermons in a studio and the healings in his tent He began building his own network to carry his programs, since the commercial networks kept his spectacular "healings" off the air. By the early 1960s Roberts was becoming tired of the constant travel, setting up his tent, pulling it down, and then starting all over again. Moreover, he realized that he reached more people through an evening's television than in a year of tent meetings. In 1967 he folded his big tent for the last time and withdrew to take stock of himself. He did retain his radio program to keep in touch with his followers.

The result was that Roberts made a number of changes in his life. He left the Pentecostal Holiness Church and became a Methodist. He decided to make his permanent base in Tulsa, Oklahoma, and began developing it. He returned to television in 1969. Ben Armstrong, in his book *The Electric Church*, describes it this way: "The sparkling new TV presentation had everything that would guarantee success for any series — bright contemporary music, attractive young people, a fast pace, superb technical quality, and a well-known personality at its center." The new program did not feature healings — these are only done at Crusade meetings. As the money poured in, sometimes accompanied by 100,000 letters a week, Roberts built a multimillion-dollar studio complex. He had also begun Oral Roberts University, which his program was to promote, using its students as choir and in other roles. His son Richard became his star singer. All in all, it was as slick as any commercially produced program.

Roberts also began his huge City of Faith Medical Center, much to the criticism of local Tulsa hospitals that were already competitive for patients and labeled his institution as unnecessary. Roberts saw his hospital as a world center of healing and poured millions of dollars into it. Time has proven the Tulsa criticism right, because the hospital has never caught on. Even the university has fallen on leaner days. In its beginning it had a basketball team that was one of the better squads in the country, but it has long since disappeared from the sports pages. Actually, in a way, the university and hospital were self-defeating because he had to devote more and more time on his program to their support, thus cutting into entertainment values and losing part of his audience. Both these institutions have kept the ministry in a continual financial crisis.

Other problems began cropping up. Roberts' son Richard, who was now claiming the power of healing, went through a publicized divorce which was difficult to justify in the light of biblical fundamentalism. A disgruntled employee went public with accusations of financial irregularities, false fund-raising techniques, and scandalous lifestyle. When television's "60 Minutes" came to Tulsa to investigate the charges, the program revealed that the ex-employee had been beaten up by goons. Oral Roberts did not help the image with some bizarre claims of visions. He reported to his audience that he had encountered and chatted with a 900-foot-high Jesus, who told him to urge people to support the medical complex. Later he went public, insisting that God had told him he would die if he failed to receive eight million dollars by a certain date. A dog-track owner from Sarasota, Florida, showed up in Tulsa with a check for a million dollars to save Roberts' life. Both stories made international headlines and brought ridicule on the ministry. Another time, as a fund-raising come-on, he sent his mailing list a piece of cloth with the imprint of his hand — the hand with the healing power. Like Falwell and Swaggart, Roberts is a millennialist who gives the impression that the end is not far distant.

Roberts pushes his healing powers through his magazine, *Abundant Life*. In it he matches all the New Testament miracles of Christ plus healing cancer. The magazine presents the idea that it is the will of God that people contribute to him and that by doing so the contributor will earn God's blessing. Like most of the televangelists he has banks of phones over which his people can hard sell, often urging his contributors to help him so that he can beat Satan, who is trying to undermine his work

and defeat God. Great effort is made to turn the occasional contributor into a regular donor, monthly preferably.

Although he does not attack the Catholic Church on his TV
programs, he does criticize Catholic ideas. Off the air, both pub-
licly and privately, he is not so considerate. As with so many
other evangelists, Roberts is convinced that the Catholic Church
is anti-biblical and thus presumably a work of Satan. He does
not have the vitriol of a Swaggart, but his condemnation is
nonetheless severe. He claims to have Catholic donors who are
beginning to see the true light.

Ernest Angley

The authors of *Prime Time Preachers* refer to the pastor of
Akron's Grace Cathedral this way: "Ernest Angley has been
called the 'lunatic fringe' of religious broadcasting. He sees demons leaving the bodies of those he heals. He sees angels, too,
standing by his side in healing services. And he sees God, who
he says looks more or less like the pictures of Him." This despite the Apostle John's assurance that no man has ever seen the
Father, who is pure spirit. Angley (pronounced "Ang" as in
"angel") has been called other such names as "unction with a
smile," "pure corn," and "unconventional." His programs lack
sophistication; he dresses as if he bought his clothes off a rack at
Goodwill; wears a toupee-looking toupee; lacks the charismatic
presence of most of his competitors, appears as a short, stubby
man, hunched over in intensity — yet he packs them in for every
service.

Ernest Angley says he met God face to face for the first time
when he was a seven-year-old boy, living on the family farm in
North Carolina. God came to him while he was in bed one night
and told him to look out the window at all the stars, promising him
that was how many souls he would win for Jesus. About his work
today, he says, "I'm a Bible preacher who gets the word of God

into people. It's harvest time. God is just sweeping them in through my crusade."

Angley's base is his "cathedral" in Akron. Here he televises his shows through Grace Cathedral and a more intimate set that resembles an ornate Victorian living room. The latter set allows him to bring on guests who plug his ministry. It also permits him to make a concerted pitch for funds. Holding up a copy of his magazine, *Holy Ghost*, which he promises to send to viewers, if they will be "a friend to Jesus and send money," he talks to the various groups who support him, stirring up his Outreach Partners: "We don't have long. Jesus is soon coming. You Partners are bringing thousands before the Lord. On that Great Day your reward will be great." His Number One Partners are those who contribute a dollar a day to his Mission for All Nations. He assures: "Send your money where it is used one hundred percent for souls. I have no bank account, take only a small salary. My wealth is in souls."

Angley holds Holy Ghost rallies at Grace Cathedral. He invites his television audience to attend. Those who cannot be present are invited to send their names. If they have not been baptized in the Holy Spirit, he promises, "I'll call the Holy Spirit down on you even if you are not here." He also says he cures over television, and as he extends his hand to the camera lens he tells his audience to touch the screen of their sets and be healed. A reporter for the *Atlanta Constitution* describes a healing session for his paper: "For the next three hours, Ernest Angley 'healed,' squealed and ranted in the name of God. A line of the afflicted formed at one side of the stage, and the faith healer attended to them, usually one at a time, laying hands upon their foreheads, casting out 'foul demons' and 'loosing' them from Satan. Many were so overcome by Angley's cathartic commands that they collapsed to the floor, 'slain in the spirit,' and rose stunned, sometimes murmuring gibberish — 'speaking in tongues.' The multitude applauded frequently, urged on by Angley: 'Give God a big hand, everybody!' " *Prime Time Preach-*

ers, which reprinted the above, adds that a woman from North Carolina died of a heart attack "moments after receiving Angley's healing touch for her weak heart."

As a fund-raiser, Angley also holds banquets around the United States and Canada. Outreach Partners are invited to attend, and for the price of a ticket he promises "a full-course meal and then laying on hands with miracles in abundance."

Angley also holds foreign crusades in the Third World which he calls "taking Jesus to the world in this final hour." He says that he doesn't select crusade sites, but God does it through a direct line to him. He confides: "I don't act through inspiration but revelation." He ties tours into these crusades and sells seats through his program, promising vast crowds and "up to a hundred thousand miracles in a service." He never fails to take along a television crew to record these "miracles" which will become fodder for his shows back home.

That people accept all this as gospel truth is evident from the crowds that he attracts both here and abroad. People who are incurably ill will grasp at any straw, and it is understandable why they come, but it is hard to understand the others who suspend all reasonable incredulity. Since most of the televangelists do not go in for healing, they are critical of Angley for his abuse of people's trust, but this does not bother the Akron prophet who outdoes even Moses in seeing and talking to God.

Other Ministries

The above ministries have been described at some length because of their great popularity. For the most part they represent preachers whose tactics are bizarre and questionable. (The Falwell ministry is an exception.) All of them revolve around a strong figure, and it is doubtful if any would last beyond their leader. This poses a serious problem because all represent a heavy investment in land, buildings, and personnel. These investments and their continuance require a hard sell. Any ministry needs the financial support of its followers, but listeners to all these men are asked to go to extremes because of the continuous need for excessive sums. The result is that there is less and less time for a scriptural message and people are reaching a saturation point.

There are other biblical messengers who would like to come into your home and whose programs are generally available throughout the United States. All of these programs center on charismatic individuals who understand the potential of television and the value of face-to-face communication. Here are some of these luminaries.

Kenneth Copeland is a Pentecostal who injects humor into his telecasts. While he advocates healing and speaking in tongues, one writer calls him "a comedian's caricature of an evangelist." He began his television ministry in 1979 and has been steadily adding stations. He is a fixture of those stations given over to Christian broadcasting. His preaching style is one of energetic movement, coupled with planned wry wit. His message is fundamental pentecostalism, and he does not like the main-line churches because they are doctrinally staid and stagnant. He sees Satan as a real person and a constant threat. On one telecast he told how he ordered Satan out of his house forever. He is a pilot who flies his own plane, from which Satan has also been exorcised. His technique is different, but it brings in the dollars.

D. James Kennedy is pastor of the Coral Ridge Presbyterian Church in Fort Lauderdale, Florida. He presents himself as an alternative to the frenetic services of the Pentecostals, whom he believes appeal to the "obviously uneducated, narrowminded, and backwoodsy." He presents a traditional service with hymns, Scripture, and sermons in which he speaks his mind. He is also a believer in political action, associating himself with the Moral Majority at the time of the Reagan campaign.

Richard De Haan on his "Day of Discovery" is more a Bible teacher than a Bible preacher. His father, M. R. De Haan, was a respected pioneer radio evangelist who began a program from Detroit in 1938 that was a Bible lesson. This grew into the Radio Bible Class, Inc., of Grand Rapids, Michigan, in which Mr. De Haan taught a Bible class every day. Members of Mr. DeHaan's parish disapproved of their pastor, a former physician, ministering outside his congregation, so he resigned and devoted full time to his radio apostolate, which was continued by his son, M. R. De Haan II. A television program was started and called "Day of Discovery," with headquarters at Cypress Gardens, Florida. Another son, Richard, directs this endeavor. It is a solid Protestant program built around the Discovery Singers, an occasional interview, and a Gospel message. The highlight of the year is the Easter Sunrise Service held at Cypress Gardens, an international tourist attraction. While the atmosphere is inspirational, there is no histrionics or dunning for money. A copy of the day's Bible lesson is offered to viewers who write in, and about a million copies are distributed monthly. Those who write in do send donations, but they are not required to do so. In addition, a Bible course is available to those who wish to purchase it. The program is supported by its regular viewers without the solicitations one finds with the flamboyant preachers.

James Robison is an evangelist who has not yet quite reached the level of the Falwells and Swaggarts. He is a fiery preacher who attended a few courses at East Texas Baptist College but never graduated. He makes his independent views known both through his television programs and his magazine, *Life's Answer*.

Robison began his career as a nineteen-year-old revival preacher, having been "saved" at the age of fifteen. He had an unhappy childhood. Deserted by his alcoholic father as an infant and unwanted by his mother, he finally found a home with a minister and his wife. What biblical knowledge he has, he picked up from his foster parents and on his own initiative. His early revivals were popular, and he was constantly in demand. He brought the style of these rural missions to his television presence. He is outspoken, ready to fight for what he believes, and his political ideas parallel those of Jerry Falwell. He gained national attention for his political activities in behalf of Ronald Reagan and the New Christian Right. Southerners who form the majority of his audience love his pulpit-pounding and condemnations. His fund-raising is hard-sell, and he offers premiums from "Vote" lapel pins and bumper stickers to crosses.

Robert Schuller is this generation's Norman Vincent Peale. Where Peale taught the virtue of positive thinking, Schuller proclaims a gospel of possibility thinking — "Believe it and you can make it happen." The Reformed Church of America, a Calvinist denomination of theological conservatism, is parent church for both men. Schuller was sent to Southern California in 1955 to start a ministry there. He began his preaching from the roof of a refreshment stand in a drive-in parking lot. Today his Garden Grove Community Church is housed in a spectacular glass-buttressed Crystal Cathedral from which Schuller's national Sunday telecasts are broadcast. He sweeps into the sanctuary each week, clad in a handsome preaching robe, arms outstretched, face beaming, and proclaiming, "This is the day the Lord has made! Let us rejoice and be glad!" His music features Hollywood singers, and his guests are mostly recognizable celebrities. Where most of the television preachers confine themselves to biblical interpretation, Schuller is concerned with the basic problems of daily life. He is an expert at coining memorable slogans. "Find a need and fill it; find a hurt and heal it!" he tells his Hour of Power audience. Critics claim that Schuller preaches nothing more than psychological do-goodism, but he defends his technique by saying that a preacher must first reach people where they are and then lead them into the message of Christ. In fact, his Sunday evening service, which is not televised, is much more doctrinal than the morning spectacular. The Hour of Power claims two million regular viewers, with the lowest number being surprisingly in the West. His strongest base is the Midwest. Schuller disassociates himself from his fundamentalist competition and goes his own way in presenting a well-planned and professionally executed telecast.

There are a number of televangelists standing in the wings and hoping their national moment will come — men such as Dean Brown and John Ankerberg (who accused Jim Bakker of homosexuality). There are also hundreds of local ministers appearing on local stations who have not yet reached out to a wider audience.

Surprisingly, although women today are being ordained ministers in greater numbers, none has made an impression in the field of televangelism. Years ago, Aimee Semple McPherson and her Four Square Gospel Church did gain national prominence. She owned a radio station and used it in her rallies to keep in contact with her followers. When she died in 1944, her ministry was badly wracked by scandal. Many years later, Katherine Kuhlman did use television to gain a national audience, but her ministry disappeared when she died in 1976, one of the defects in personality ministries.

The Religious Talk Shows

The PTL Club

As this is being written, the PTL Club is still on the air, limping badly but making desperate efforts to hold what audience it has left. Whether it will survive the loss of its creator,

Jim Bakker, and the scandal he caused is yet to be seen. In any case, the PTL shows what one man can build up in the way of schmaltz under the guise of religion and what happens to such a ministry when its charismatic leader is brought down.

Jim Bakker was born into an Assemblies of God family of Muskegon, Michigan, where his father was a factory worker. His boyhood was marred by his small size, making him reserved and defensive. He began studying for the Assemblies of God ministry at North Central Bible College but dropped out to marry. Despite this educational lack, he was later granted ministerial credentials. With his wife, Tammy Fay, he took to the road as a traveling evangelist, making one-night stands throughout the Midwest, practicing faith healing, and speaking in tongues. Jim and Tammy developed a puppet act to teach the Bible which came to the attention of Pat Robertson, who in 1965 was looking for a children's show for his struggling Christian Broadcasting Network in Virginia Beach, Virginia. Jim and Tammy Fay were hired and began appearing on the air. Robertson was under continual pressure for funds and, as a fund-raising device, called for 700 viewers to pledge ten dollars each month to keep CBN afloat. The response was good and gave Bakker an idea. Why not start a program called the 700 Club which would air daily as a talk and inspirational show and at the same time be a constant reminder for the need of funds?

Robertson bought the idea, and in 1966 the 700 Club went on the air with Bakker as its Jack Paar. The program caught on and became the mainstay of CBN, bringing in new viewers and growing support. What led Bakker to break with Robertson is not clear. Both men say the parting was amicable. At any rate, Bakker left CBN and went to California to work for Paul Crouch's Trinity Broadcasting Network. Here Bakker introduced a new show, called Praise The Lord, patterned after his successful 700 Club. It also caught on. However, Crouch and his wife, Jan, did not like being upstaged by an employee, and before long there was a falling out. Bakker received an invitation from some laymen from Charlotte, North Carolina, to begin a ministry there. He couldn't take Praise The Lord, since it belonged to Crouch, but he did take the PTL initials and began the PTL Club, explaining that the initials stood for People That Love. However, when the program became successful, he began reverting to the original title which he believed belonged to him.

The PTL ministry began with a single station in Charlotte in 1974, but within four years was playing on over 200 stations nationwide. Bakker proved a very innovative fund-raiser, and the money rolled in. He had evolved a tremendously successful technique of weeping while making an appeal, beginning this method on the 700 Club and learning that when it was used it set every phone in the network's bank of phones ringing. Money gave him the wherewithal for expansion, and state-of-the-art studios were built that used every modern technique down to its satellite dishes. He began the Heritage School of Evangelism, which taught evangelism and communication, using the studio facilities (and getting free help), which was intended to expand into Heritage University. He built a Disney-like Heritage Theme Park, including a high-rise hotel with a suite for himself and Tammy right out of *The Arabian Nights*.

The way money was being used brought on criticism. In Charlotte the network was being referred to as Pass The Loot. A Charlotte newspaper and several radio stations began their own investigations. Accusations were made that money raised for missionary purposes and other causes was being diverted into Bakker projects and high living. The ministry provided Bakker and his family with a million-dollar five-level house which it called a parsonage. The master bedroom had his-and-her bathroom suites, connected by a sunken whirlpool tub, flanked by a glass-enclosed rock garden. There was a 600-square-foot closet for Tammy Fay to keep her clothes. The house had a music room where Tammy Fay could practice her singing and write songs for the recordings the ministry pushed.

There was also a small gymnasium. When he was queried about all this luxury, Bakker's simple response was that God wanted him to have it.

All of these facts and rumors finally came to the attention of the Federal Communications Commission, which in 1979 charged PTL with diverting money from purposes for which it was collected. Threatened with the loss of tax exemption, Bakker fought back over the air, likening the FCC to a satanic force out to destroy God's work. He accused the FCC of "witch hunting" and "fishing," calling on his followers to protest. The FCC was deluged with angry letters from his listeners. The FCC pulled in its horns — which was in a way unfortunate for Bakker because it left him free for the debacle that was to come. Even after Jimmy Swaggart exposed Bakker for sexual irregularity, and John Ankerberg added charges of homosexuality at the ministry, Bakker still held on to a hard core of loyal followers. However, it was all too much for the Assemblies of God, so he was euchred out of the ministry and Falwell took over.

Those who know Bakker expect him to come back in a new ministry, full of repentance, weeping over his sins, and they expect that the tears will win out once again.

The 700 Club

There are three separate entities centered in Virginia Beach, Virginia, all under control of Pat Robertson: the Christian Broadcasting Network; its mainstay program, the 700 Club; and the CBN cable service. the first two are tax-exempt organizations, while the last is a for-profit corporation. They are all housed in colonial-style red brick buildings that give more the impression of a college than a television studio.

Marion G. "Pat" Robertson, the creator of all this, comes from an old-line political and religious family. Born in Lexington, Virgina, in 1930, Robertson was the second son of U.S. Senator A. Willis Robertson. His mother, Gladys Churchill

Robertson, was the daughter of a fundamentalist minister, a distributor of religious tracts, and the one who passed on that old-time religion to her children. Robertson attended McAllie School in Tennessee, graduated Phi Beta Kappa from Washington and Lee University, and then from Yale University Law School; he did not pass the New York bar exam and thus has never practiced law. In 1950 his Marine Reserve unit was called up and sent to Korea, where he landed in cushy jobs and never saw combat. Years later a former congressman, who knew him in Korea, accused him of pulling political strings to keep out of the fighting. Robertson filed a libel suit but later withdrew it, saying the pressures of his political campaign prevented him from giving the case the attention it needed.

After the war Robertson went into the electronic component business, also serving as an economic consultant to W. R. Grace Co. In 1954 he married Adelia Elmer, ten weeks before the birth of the first of their four children. That boy, Tim, is now his father's right hand and host of the 700 Club. Up to this point, Robertson was not overly religious. A meeting with a Dutch evangelist led him to reevaluate his life, and he left his pregnant wife to make a retreat in the Canadian woods. When he emerged, he enrolled in New York Theological Seminary, graduating in 1959. At the seminary he had adopted Pentecostal practices, such as speaking in tongues and faith healing. For a time he and his family lived in a charismatic commune in Brooklyn, New York. Then in 1961 he heard about a broken-down UHF television station that was for sale in Virginia Beach. He managed to put a seventy-dollar down payment on it and spoke in area churches raising donations to buy it. Ben Armstrong of the National Religious Broadcasters called at the station not long after it went on the air and reported, "When I visited WYAH-TV, I certainly didn't ever expect it to amount to much. The studio looked like something put together with coat hangers. I wondered how anyone could have the audacity to think he could have a real live program under these condi-

tions!" When not too many years later the Religious Broadcasters Association gave its Award of Merit to Pat Robertson for ex-
cellence, he was operating TV stations in Atlanta, Dallas, and
Portsmouth, with radio stations in Norfolk, Albany, Syracuse,
Elmira, Rochester, and Buffalo.

Robertson built his present empire out of the 700 Club,
which as already mentioned rose from a fund-raising effort.
Through the Club Pat Robertson preached his philosophy:
"The more you give to God, the more He will give back to
you." Today the 700 Club airs three times a day over the CBN
cable network. Between these showings the network features
old reruns of family-oriented commercial TV shows — from
"Father Knows Best" to "Wagon Train." Although Robertson
has made some extravagant claims on the 700 Club when he
was host, the program avoids the fire-and-brimstone oratory of
a Swaggart or Roberts. It aims to be non-denominational, and
has taken on the look of a magazine rather than a talk show.
The station maintains banks of phones where "saved" callers
are referred to a local church by counselors. Robertson said the
people who call the station and its counselors across the country
represent main-line Protestants, Catholics, and Jews, because
"everybody appreciates being prayed for." Robertson himself
has a good television presence, projecting the image of a happy,
gracious, educated man, interested in his guests.

The Robertson complex is located on a 720-acre tract that,
besides the multimillion-dollar studio complex, includes a university with an enrollment of about one thousand. CBN em-
ploys eleven hundred people. The televangelist scandals, which
financially hurt all ministries, dropped 700 Club income thirty-
two percent and a few employees had to be let go. The cable network, however, which accepts advertising has had a steady
growth in profit. The CBN network leaned over backwards to
remain neutral in the Robertson campaign for the presidency,
not even sending a camera crew to tape its founder. Tim Robertson explained: "It might cause some confusion in the public's

mind about the role of CBN. We decided not to mention the race. Also, because the Christian Broadcasting Network is a nonprofit organization, we might risk our tax-exempt status."

Political insiders expect Robertson to make another try for the presidential nomination, again using his audience of the 700 Club as his base. However, they also expect him to be more cautious on the air since in the past campaign unrehearsed remarks made in interviews came back to haunt him. Robertson resigned his ministry to run for the nomination in 1988 and said he emphatically resented continual reference to him as a televangelist and wanted to be called simply a television executive. After withdrawing from the presidential race, he returned to his television ministry.

Catholics and the Televangelists

Should Catholics tune into these broadcasts? It depends. Some are innocuous, like Robert Schuller's Rotarianism, which can boost one's spirit, or like Billy Graham's fundamental scriptural approach. Others are subtly and not so subtly in opposition to the Catholic Church. Still others are pure quackery. The immediate danger in many telecasts is in accepting teaching that is very narrow and aimed to condition the uncritical viewer. It also contributes to the widespread opinion among so many Americans that one religion is as good as another. Most of these broadcasts share God's truth in varying degrees, but it is also difficult for the unschooled to recognize where truth ends and where the evangelist's personal opinion begins, and this can be confusing to faith. It is my own opinion that the risks to faith do not justify the small benefits gained.

Moreover, while what is said may not contradict Catholic belief, it is in what is *not* said that makes these programs woefully deficient. One hears nothing about such basic Catholic teachings as the nature and authority of the Church, the Sacraments (particularly the Eucharist), and the saints (particularly the Virgin Mary). You will not hear a systematic discussion of the Creed, private and liturgical prayer, the Fathers and Doctors of the Church, Catholic prayers such as the Rosary, the Councils of the Church, and so on — all the riches of Catholic life are ignored.

It is recognized that many Catholics are hungry for the word of God, more than they get in a ten-minute Sunday homily, and for this reason reach out to televangelists. This is a challenge to Catholic bishops and religious institutes. There are a few Catholic programs, such as The Christophers and Insight and a few individual ministries, but these are dependent on the charity of donated time and as such are relegated to unsalable hours when very few are watching or listening. Mother Angelica is attempting to set up her own network but is reached by too few and gets little support from the official Church. There are a few diocesan efforts. The Diocese of St. Petersburg has a high-powered around-the-clock radio station, WBVM, that effectively proclaims God's message. Some dioceses have closed-circuit TV and the resultant limited viewers.

There is an annual national Catholic communications collection, with half the funds applied locally and the other half ineffective nationally. Years ago, in donated time, the Catholic Hour was carried over radio and developed a following with such outstanding speakers as the late Fulton J. Sheen and Father James Gillis. Until it is realized that the Church must purchase an hour of weekly time and produce programs equal in quality and personality with the popular televangelists, the Church will have no national presence in a medium that is so effective. If Pat Robertson can develop a 700 Club and out of it build the Christian Broadcasting Network with studios and satellites, it is difficult to believe that the Catholic Church with all its resources cannot do likewise if the will is present.

11

The Local Cults

A CROSS THE COUNTRY in cities and towns, local cults
have developed, centered on a charismatic father figure
who has his own ideas of biblical interpretation and church, using peer pressure to attact youthful converts. While these cults
gain no national exposure, they can be exceedingly upsetting to
parents who lose children to them and disturbing to orthodox
local pastors, who are unable to compete with them. They go
under self-coined names, such as The Navigators, Apostolic
Church of Jesus, Faith Assembly, Faith Mission, Calvary Community Church, Square Gospel Tabernacle, Jesus Fellowship,
Faith Miracle Center, Open Door, Community Bible Church,
and so on. The story of how one of these cults developed is typical of most of them.

William David Winn III was born in Dania, Florida, in
1956. Early on, his family moved to Miami, where he was
brought up. His father was a railroad employee, his mother a
homemaker. The family was Episcopal, and Winn was raised
in that faith. He now says that he found the Episcopal Church
sterile and stopped going in his teens. When he was eighteen, he
joined the Air Force and eventually found himself stationed at
MacDill AFB at the southern end of the Tampa peninsula. A
fellow NCO began talking to him about the Bible, whetting
Winn's interest, and inviting him to attend Calvary Community

Church, a fundamentalist group in Tampa, Florida. Before long, he was active in the ministry of the church, and when his enlistment ran out, he did not "re-up" but opted to work in the ministry efforts of Calvary Community.

Winn, a handsome, stocky, intense man, chose to make his ministry at the University of South Florida. He was regularly seen outside the U.S.F. library talking to students, and in time recruited a few followers. He and his small group distributed Bibles and tracts on campus and won converts to Calvary Community. In 1987 Winn and the church pastor had a falling out. Winn says the pastor was jealous of his success at U.S.F. and angered because Winn would not complete studies for a degree from the pastor's Tampa Bay Bible College. The pastor, on the other hand, said Winn was disruptive at the Bible college, refused to wear a tie to school, drank coffee during classes, and was unorganized and non-conformist in his ministry. Winn responds, "A person to serve the Lord does not need formal training or a degree or nothing." He withdrew from the church.

Winn set up a real estate business in order to support his wife and young son and sought for ways to continue his campus ministry. He approached the pastor of the Northside Bible Church in Lutz, a Tampa suburb, but was told the church had no room for him. In order to continue his Bible work, he appointed one of his converts, Joy Reed, to manage the real estate office. Reed had come to the University of South Florida from Brooklyn to prepare for a career in dentistry. She met Winn and several followers outside the university library when she came out for a break. Winn recruited her into the group and she left school and her planned career. As office manager, Reed does as much to sell the Bible as she does to sell her real estate. One of her converts there was Andrew Maldonado, a New Yorker, who had done eight months in a New Jersey prison for attempted murder and who had come to Tampa to settle. She gave him a talk on the Bible and a tract on heaven and won him to Winn's cause.

Winn decided to begin his own church, named it Community Bible Church, rented a five-bedroom house in Lutz, where he installed his family and followers and which was to be the beginning of a missionary training facility, rooted in his interpretation of the Bible. Winn says his mission is patterned on early Christian churches. The recruits, who have outside jobs, turn their earnings over to the community, call Winn "Dad," and he calls them "Son" and "Daughter." Time in the house is spent in Bible study and prayer sessions. No secular books, television, radio, newspapers, or record albums (even Gospel music) are allowed.

Winn's activities have not gone unnoticed in the Tampa press. A theft charge was filed against him by the county attorney in response to a complaint by a former member that Winn had kept possession of her personal computer and books. He made the papers again when he became embroiled in a dispute with his landlord, who had become concerned about the number of people living in the house and wanted to inspect it. Winn would not allow him on the premises.

The biggest contretemps so far has been a running feud between Winn and Hillsborough Community College which several times has had to get the police to force him off campus. Winn had converted two players from the University of South Florida tennis team. After the girls graduated they took jobs as coaches for the HCC tennis program and began preaching Winn's teachings to the students, forming a prayer group of players. Winn began coming on campus to give Bible teaching at the tennis courts. College officials objected to religious services being held on school property and during school hours. The police had to be called several times to end the sessions. The parents of two of the HCC tennis players Winn had recruited came and, according to Winn, "kidnapped" their daughters. Again the police became involved and contacted the girls, both from out of state, and after interviewing them dropped the investigation. One of the coaches also withdrew from the movement over the fuss Winn was making.

Whether Community Bible Church will last is yet to be seen. So far Winn has shown great talent in making converts to his cause but has not shown equal skill in raising money, which will be necessary for growth. He has gathered a devoted group of young people who make great sacrifices for him, much to the consternation of many parents who believe their children have been brainwashed. Winn has almost no scholarly knowledge of the Bible, but that has not stopped others from developing their own cult of followers.

The Winn story is told here because it is typical of how these local cults start. These movements are generally unknown and undescribed. Very often concerned parents inquire about them, but there is very little that can be told since they are only known locally. The Winn story should be a warning to young people who are away from home, at college, or in military camps. They should be aware that there are peers among them who would like to win their minds and recruit them for the cause of some spiritual guru. Often homesick and lonely, with some acquaintances but rarely a friend, they are already set up for the recruiter who shows an interest in them. Introduced to a "family" like Winn's and taken in by a smile and pleasant manner, they are prime targets to be separated from their real families and their career choices in order to establish a "personal relationship with God," who all too often turns out to be not God but a William David Winn or a Sun Myung Moon.

12

The Way

THE CULT'S recruiting meeting was not announced with a great fanfare. The sign on the college bulletin board simply read:

Worried?
Learn how to kick the habit
Room 211   4 PM

Those who attend the meeting will learn that the answers to any problems they have will be found in The Way. They won't be told that The Way is a cult seeking total control over them. Instead they will meet some seemingly loving and caring people who want to share with them a way of life, supposedly from New Testament times. The Way will house and shelter them, teach them the "true" meaning of the Bible, enable them to speak in tongues. They will not be told that once they are in the movement they will have to turn everything they own over to it, that they will spend their time hawking The Way publications, selling courses in its founder's teachings, called *Power for Abundant Living*, and enrolling new recruits.

The Way International was founded by Victor Paul Wierwille, who was born in 1916 in New Knoxville, Ohio, where the group now has its headquarters. Wierwille boasted of extensive theological and scriptural education, but all that can be proven are some correspondence courses from Moody Bible

Institute in Chicago and a degree from a Western diploma mill where anyone can purchase a diploma by simply paying a fee. Wierwille began as an Evangelical and Reformed minister in Van Wert, Ohio. He tells how, when he was praying, God "spoke to me audibly, just like I am talking to you now. He said He would teach me the Word as it has not been known since the first century if I would teach it to others." Most of "what God taught him" was to be taken from the works of E. W. Bullinger, particularly *How to Enjoy the Bible* and *The Giver and His Gifts*. He burned his theological books and began developing his own way through Scripture. This led him into conflict with his church, and he resigned in 1958 and began organizing The Way.

Joel A. MacCollam, who has made a detailed study of the movement, describes its organization in this way: "Followers are tightly organized on the model of a tree. The tree's trunk is the International Headquarters at New Knoxville, Ohio. The board of directors is the root; the state organization is the limb; city-wide or regional ministries are the branches; the local fellowship in a home or on campus is the twig; and each believer is the leaf. The Way places its strongest emphasis on the twig level, and it is here that the group's theological exclusivenesss, coupled with strong peer pressure to 'band together' in worship and fellowship, as well as the accepted status of Way ministers as ordained clergy, combine to suggest that The Way does indeed function as a church."

The Way calls itself a Christian movement, but it is no more Christian than Jehovah's Witnesses or the Mormons, falling into the same error as those sects in denying the divinity of Jesus. Wierwille, in his book *Jesus Christ Is Not God*, calls Jesus the son of God but not God the Son. "Show me one place in the Bible where it says He is God," Wierwille challenges in resurrecting a third-century heresy and ignoring New Testament passages that identify Jesus with the Father. To prove his allegations, Wierwille makes interpolations in the Bible, badly mistranslating (among others) the opening verses of the Gospel of John to justify his teaching. Thus in denying the divinity of Jesus, The Way also denies the Trinity, which we have shown earlier is a fundamental Christian doctrine that these cults have difficulty with.

Wierwille also teaches that the Gospels were written in Aramaic, when any scholar could tell him that the original language was Greek. He dismisses the Old Testament as being extraneous and says the four Gospels belong to the Old Testament (thus in effect making them unmeaningful). Only Acts and the Pauline epistles are to be counted. He mixes up the words "soul" and "spirit," which in Christian terminology mean the same but to Wierwille are two different things. He teaches that Adam and Eve were body, soul, and spirit but lost their "spirit" in the Fall and then became just body and soul as any other animal, and that as a result no person had a spirit until after Pentecost and that proof of having a spirit is in speaking in tongues. To teach that there is life after death, according to The Way guru, is to propagate a life of Satan. He pays no heed to sins committed in "body and soul" because the real sin can only be committed in "spirit." Some ex-members of The Way say that Wierwille's teaching on sin results in justifying acts condemned in Scripture by saying the sin was in body and soul and not in the "born again" spirit. While Wierwille counterfeits Christianity, it is a counterfeit that can be easily recognized by comparing it with the original.

In 1982 Wierwille retired from active direction of the movement. Cult watchers expected his son, Don, an elementary schoolteacher, to succeed him; but the founder, unpredictable as ever, named an assistant, Rev. Craig Martindale, to head up the movement. Don was made head of The Way College in Emporia, Kansas, which trains twig leaders. The group has its own publishing house, American Christian Press, to produce *The Way Magazine*, Wierwille books, and Way courses. There are other training centers in Indiana and California.

The Way continues to promote itself as a Bible study group, but any parents who have lost a child to the movement know very well that it is a cult. Should a twig leader or "leaf" approach you with an invitation to a campus study group, remember the old spiritual axiom: "Resist beginnings." Once in and brainwashed, one finds it is very difficult to get out. Many people do eventually leave the cult, but they have lost productive years of their lives before escaping and regaining religious sanity.

13

East Meets West

SINCE THE END of World War II, various Eastern religions have invaded the United States, spreading their teachings under calculated disguises. Today one can find Buddhist temples in many parts of the country. There are other temples to strange Indian gods. Muslim mosques shelter Islamic imams who teach the laws of Muhammad. Some of these came into being to serve foreign populations that had emigrated to the United States, while others were founded to gain native American converts. Success has not been inconsiderable. In 1959 an Indian guru, Maharishi Mahesh Yogi, arrived in the United States to found the Spiritual Rejuvenation Movement that would teach a yogic technique he called transcendental meditation and before long had several million adherents being introduced to Indian mysticism. These meditators even included simplistic priests and nuns who did not realize that they were being initiated into Hindu pantheism. The Muslim movement gained a strong foothold in the American black community, largely as a protest movement against whites. An Eastern fraud named Bhagwan Shree Rajneesh built a commune that controlled a western county and was making serious inroads in a Northwestern state until irregularities led to his deportation. The success of these and many other groups shows that many Americans are drawn to esoteric religions. Several of these sects are here mentioned separately because of their vigorous methods of proselytizing young Americans.

Baha'i

This Persian heresy of Shiite Muslimism began when a twenty-four-year-old rug merchant took the title of Bab and proclaimed himself a greater prophet than Muhammad, one sent by God to reform Islam. He was persecuted by orthodox Muslims, and several rebellions he began were savagely put down. After one of them he was arrested and executed. Before his death in 1850 he had predicted that a greater prophet than he would arise. In 1863 one of Bab's followers, Baha'u'llah, proclaimed himself that prophet and, taking direction of the movement, he wrote a book of laws, *The Most Holy Book*, which became the infallible Baha'i bible. He died in 1892, was buried in what is now Israel, and was succeeded by his son, Abdul-Baha, who spread the new religion to Europe. When he died in 1921, he willed the movement to his Oxford-educated grandson, who died in 1957 without heirs. Since that time the movement has been governed by a nine-person infallible board, known as the Universal House of Justice, from its Haifa, Israel, headquarters. Today the movement has spread throughout the world, making great inroads in Africa. It is also growing in the United States, recruiting widely on college campuses, and has built an enormous temple that dominates the skyline of Wilmette, Illinois, which is also its center for this country. However, in Iran under Khomeini, Baha'is are still being persecuted and murdered.

The basic tenet of the new faith is that God has made Himself known to man through various manifestations over the centuries, chiefly through His prophets — Abraham, Moses, Jesus Christ, Muhammad, Bab and Baha'u'llah. Baha'i teaches the unity of all religions, advocates universal education, world peace, the equality of men and women, one international language, and one international government. These general aims are attractive to many Americans, drawing them into Baha'i meetings. The Baha'i literature here makes frequent mention of Jesus in order to attract Christian converts. It is only after they are solidly in the faith that more esoteric doctrines are shared and Baha'u'llah's teachings take precedence over all others — the Bible, the Koran, or whatever one formerly believed. However, since Baha'ism is rooted in Islam, Jesus is not God or the Son of God, but simply one in a long line of prophets, whose teachings must be judged against those of the infallible Baha'i bible. Christ died as so many other martyrs did, Baha'i teaches, and His death has no theological significance; of course, He did not literally arise from the dead, but only through His teachings. Thus they take the heart out of Christian belief in the redemptive sacrifice of Jesus, the nature of sin, and His resurrection. The Baha'is say that a person can give allegiance to both Jesus and Baha'u'llah, but for anyone who understands Christianity that is not possible. The Baha'is do not exercise the mind control one finds in the cults, and it is easy to resign from the group. However, through their clubs, concerts, rock groups (including such Baha'i stars as Seals and Crofts), they present themselves as a sort of Up With The People group that can be very attractive to young adults, particularly if they are undiscriminating.

Hare Krishna

When Hare Krishnas first began proselytizing in the United States, they were a common sight on many big-city streets, with shaved heads, dancing in their yellow robes to the beat of tambourines and cymbals, begging for the support of their cause. They are still begging, but their approach is much more subtle. It may be a young girl in an airport corridor, pressing flowers on passersby for a donation, or a neatly dressed young man (wearing a wig to hide the shaven head) selling Hare Krishna books outside a local shopping mall. When these emissaries spot a young person who could be a subject for recruitment, they will try to engage that person in conversation. However, where they are in sufficient numbers, they will still come out from their ashrams and temples, dancing in yellow robes and intoning their chants, to celebrate Hindu festivals in public parks. To many Americans the Hare Krishnas look like a weird group, but to their many recruits from main-line churches this Hindu sect has a very positive appeal.

There is a pantheon of gods in the Hindu religion, not all of them pretty. The three main ones are Brahma (the creator), Shiva (the destroyer), and Vishnu, now recognized as the supreme god who has had many incarnations (avatars). One of these incarnations was as Krishna, conqueror of demons, teacher, and lover. It is not our purpose here to go into the intricacies of Hindu mythology, as populous as any Roman or Greek pantheon, but merely to show the origin of this Eastern invasion into America. In the fifteenth century, Caitanya, a Bengalese Brahmin, taught that the avatar Krishna was even greater than his source, Vishnu. J. Isamu Yamamoto, who has made a study of this sect, describes its development this way: "Since he was an exponent of *bhakti* (the way of devotion), Caitanya danced and chanted the name of Krishna in the streets. The direct love of Krishna, he taught, was the surest way to burn off ignorance and karma (the consequences of past actions) and attain bliss. Because Caitanya worshipped exclusively by chanting, singing, and dancing, however, orthodox Brahmins reproved him for being frivolous. Nevertheless, his argumentative brilliance and personal charisma attracted many followers who worshipped him as the incarnation of Krishna." This sect of Caitanya was confined to Bengal until modern times.

In 1936 a Caitanya follower, a man named Abhay Charan, was commissioned to carry these teachings to the West. He began publishing an English magazine, *Back to Godhead,* which had considerable success. In 1965 at the age of seventy, this swami carried Krishna teachings to the United States, appearing one day in Tompkins Park on the Lower East Side of New York, chanting his mantra and making his first bid for converts. This mantra was one the Krishnas still chant seemingly endlessly every day: "Hare Krishna, Hare Krishna, Krishna Krishna, Hare Hare, Hare Rama, Hare Rama, Rama Rama, Hare Hare." The first two words became the American name for the sect, although its official title is International Society for Krishna Consciousness (ISKCON).

Charan, then having the name Prabhupada (meaning "at whose feet the masters sit"), died in 1977, leaving behind eleven initiating gurus to carry on the movement, which by then had thousands of American monks, located in sixty-eight ashrams, schools, temples, and farming communities. The movement was wealthy with income from the magazine, book royalties, and gifts from such prominent people as the Beatle George Harrison, who gave a share of his royalties, and Alfred Ford, a great-grandson of Henry Ford.

Krishnas often confuse Christians by admitting in their introductory remarks that they love Jesus Christ. When asked who was the Father of Christ, they will reply, "Krishna." That is as close as they get to Christianity. The aim of the Krishna devotee is to arrive at nirvana, becoming one with Krishna. This is accomplished through a series of reincarnations and transmigrations, and in each working to improve one's karma, i.e., one's state in life as the result of actions in past incarnations. One must work in this life to improve future incarnations, for only when one has atoned sufficiently for past lives and rid himself of all attachments to the world can he cease the cycles of rebirth. This requires practicing daily devotions, chanting the Krishna mantra, meditating on the divine action of Krishna, worshiping a bush of Indian basil, thought to be of divine origin, and worshiping before deity statues that are presented with food, flowers, incense, washed and "put to bed" at night.

The life of a Hare Krishna is not an easy one. He or she is carefully brainwashed and persuaded to give up all contact with family. The initiate is moved around from temple to temple or farm to ashram, working about the residence, out begging funds for the movement, spending hours of worship and chanting, having a vegetarian diet, with few breaks in routine. In some centers of the sect, criminal actions have taken place and been brought to the attention of the police. At one temple the head guru was arrested for complicity in murder. Despite the grinding life, it is very difficult to convert members of the sect who seem totally indoctrinated and subject to their elders. Yet the love of Christ tells us that we must reach out to them, not to belittle their strange Eastern teachings, but to show them that God loves them in a very personal way and that they are not condemned to an endless recycling but to one life that never really ends.

Unification Church (Moonies)

The recruitment and fund-raising methods of the Unification Church are very similar to those of the Hare Krishnas. You will find the church's neatly dressed converts in airport corridors and waiting rooms, in shopping malls and on the street corners. They have been known to go through office buildings, floor by floor, until removed by building security. Their neat dress and friendly manner invite people to talk to them. Besides their begging, they seek out young people like themselves, telling these prospects that they have the way to meet their personal needs in a family atmosphere, but not at first revealing that the family is the Unification Church.

The Unification Church (formally, The Holy Spirit Association for the Unification of World Christianity) is the creation of Sun Myung Moon, whose original name was Yong

Myung Moon, but since Yong means "dragon," he felt it inappropriate in his new calling and adopted the Sun character for "goodness." Moon was born in 1920 into a Presbyterian farming family in what is now North Korea. He attended primary school in his home village of Kwangju and was sent to Seoul for high school. A lonesome teenager far away from home for the first time, he joined a Pentecostal church. He says he was sixteen when he was visited by Jesus and told that he had been chosen to complete the unfinished work of Christ. During World War II, Moon was in Tokyo, studying electrical engineering at Waseda University.

Moon returned to Peng Yang, Korea, and gathered a few disciples from a Pentecostal community there. He retired to a monastery, set up by a self-proclaimed Korean messiah, and formulated his teaching, later publishing it in the book *Divine Principle*. After six months he emerged and began preaching. He was arrested and imprisoned by the North Korean communists for anticommunism (according to Moon) or for bigamy (according to Korean sources). When he was released or escaped from prison, he went to the south, just in time to avoid the closing of the border between North and South Korea. He settled in the port of Pusan, there found a job as a dock laborer, and spent his spare time preaching his new religion. According to whom one believes, he invented an air gun or obtained a prototype from his disciple, Hye Won Yoo, and that was the beginning of his industrial fortune. Again scandal surrounded him. His wife left him, she says for adultery, but Moon says because "she could not comprehend my mission."

Moon came to the United States in 1971 to proclaim his new religion, calling on Americans to abandon their denominational religions and prepare for the Second Coming of Christ. He said that the New Kingdom of Heaven and Earth would begin in 1981 and we would see the Lord of the Second Advent. (When this did not happen in 1981, he advanced the date to 2001.) That his church was meeting with some success was shown by the fact that in 1981 he married 10,000 couples, 2,085 in a televised ceremony in Madison Square Garden. Moon bought a large estate in a New York suburb, a Christian Brothers' training college for a seminary of his own, a bank, the Hotel New Yorker, various industrial developments, a fishery, and properties across the United States. All of this activity attracted the attention of the Internal Revenue Service, and he was charged with tax evasion, tried, convicted, fined, and sent to prison for a year and a half. Another rumor, never proven, was that Moon was backed by the Korean CIA and had Korean government money behind him.

Moon is very media-conscious, despite the fact that the news media have been highly critical. *Time* magazine reported: "In essence, Moon's theology makes wide use of biblical personae and events, but is no more than nominally Christian. Added ingredients are an odd mixture: occultism, electrical engineering, Taoist dualism, pop sociology, and opaque metaphysical jargon." *Time* left out Moon's fascination with numerology. To offset this bad publicity, Moon organized expensive seminars for his people and Christian theologians, paying all expenses, and hosting them in such attractive places as Hawaii, Athens, and Lisbon. He underwrote major motion pictures, including one on the life of Douglas MacArthur. He founded the Washington *Times*, the only alternative voice to the liberal *Post*. He also established subgroups to attract publicity and converts; these subgroups include New Hope Singers, Korean Folk Ballet, American Youth for a Just Peace, Conference on Unified Science, and International Cultural Foundation.

The doctrine taught by Moon is quite convoluted and difficult for a mind not trained in Eastern dualism (yang and yin principle) to understand. For example, there are three Adams. The first was Adam, who had as his companion his sister, Eve, who in turn fell into sexual sin with Lucifer. The second Adam is Jesus Christ, a failure. The third Adam is the Lord of the Second Advent, presumably Moon himself. Cain was born, not the son of Adam, but of Lucifer. Jesus was supposed to unite the world into one religion, and to prepare for this unification God sent Buddha and Confucius to the Asian world and Socrates to the West to ready the way for the Messiah. But all this was foiled by John the Baptist, who brought about the crucifixion by persuading the Jews not to believe in Jesus. The distortions in Scripture are obvious and typical. To go into detail of Unification teachings is too involved and would only confuse the reader. They can be found in *Divine Practice* and can be examined against basic Christian teachings. However, if you do get into a discussion with a Moonie, remember an earlier admonition to get people to define their terms. The Moonies use Christian words but mean something quite different from your understanding.

God: God is a male-female principle (yang and yin), with the Father as male principle and the Holy Spirit as female, who gives birth to children of goodness (*Divine Principle* 215).

Jesus: Jesus did not redeem us through His death (*DP* 147-448), was not divine but a "perfected man" (*DP* 209-211), did not rise physically from the dead but as a "spirit being" (*DP* 360). Jesus failed in His mission to unite the world by finding a perfect mate and begetting a perfect family, and now this must be done through the Second Lord of the Advent (*DP* 368), who will be born in Korea (*DP* 520).

The definitions above give a sampling of Moon's teaching and show its departure from basic Christian theology. Of course, it is not revealed in the beginning to the prospective convert, but the use of Christian terms leads the neophytes to believe they are in a Christian movement. They are gradually taken through a thought-control process that convinces them that all outside the movement are under the influence of the Devil, who works particularly through those closest to you — parents and siblings — whose influence must particularly be avoided. You are taught to give your full devotion to Father (Moon) and work for his blessing. To gain this you must bring three "spiritual children" into the Unification Church, after which you will have attained perfection and be given a perfect mate to wed and bring children into the world because marriage is a necessity for salvation. You are sent to recruit in colleges and main-line churches. All you have to do is invite the prospect to the center for a meal and songfest and the leaders will do the rest. Thus the cycle is repeated.

Again, as noted previously, accept the sincerity of the Moonie and believe he or she is honestly looking for God and His Church. On the recognition of this fact, show the Moonie where truth really lies: in the Bible and in the Church. Point out that God does have a plan for us which He brought to fruition in His Son, Jesus Christ, who alone is our Savior and Teacher.

14

Finale

THIS BOOK has not been all-inclusive. There are movements we have ignored, such as Scientology, Divine Light Mission, Eckankar, Worldwide Church of God, or The Family of Love. What we have tried to present here are the main groups that come to your door, enter the home through television, or approach you in a public place. It could be objected that most of the television ministries that were described should not be lumped in the same book as such aberrant cults as Hare Krishnas or Moonies. It has not been our purpose to make them all equal, only to stress that they are all out to capture you in one way or another, and they do have certain things in common:

Missionary Zeal. The active participants in these movements are marked by missionary zeal. All of them are out to win you to their side, and all seek your financial support to spread their message, not only here in the United States but abroad, with many of the televangelists concentrating on Latin America, where the Catholic Church has been steadily losing members to Mormons, Witnesses, and Pentecostal fundamentalist sects. Anyone who has followed Swaggart telecasts has seen his revival meetings in Latin America, where he spoke to packed stadiums, converting people who were already Christians but who are told that they were in a false church and unable to be saved

135

unless they are born again in the particular doctrines of the preacher of the moment.

Charismatic Leadership. All of them have been founded under the guidance of a strong charismatic leader whose views are not questioned by his followers. This is not necessarily bad, but it embodies two dangers: first, people can be more easily led astray; and second, the movement can very well die with the loss of its leader. We have seen that happen with such ministries as those of Aimee Semple McPherson or Billy Sunday, and it now seems to be happening with the Worldwide Church of God since the death of its founder, Herbert W. Armstrong. The danger with charismatic leadership is that it doesn't generate or want internal competition, and as a result no lasting structure is built. The Mormons and Witnesses avoided this fault by establishing a hierarchy of their own. But one wonders what will happen to Jerry Falwell's ministry when a successor, not as charismatic as he, comes along and has to support all that Falwell has built. Also many of these leaders claim a direct line to heaven, whether it is God speaking to Ernest Angley, or Jesus to Oral Roberts and Jimmy Swaggart, or the Archangel Michael to Joseph Smith, or Jesus paying a visit to Sun Myung Moon — claims which their followers never question.

Strict Discipline. If we leave the televangelists aside, the other movements described here impose strict discipline. I have had an excommunicated Mormon describe what a shattering experience excommunication was for him, particularly since he lived in Utah where so much revolved around the Mormon Church. Shunning is a most powerful weapon against dissidents. I have read accounts of disfellowshipped Witnesses who found themselves cut off from communication with their natural families. There have been a number of civil suits by former Scientologists, claiming persecution by the church they had left. Do not underestimate this as a bar to conversion.

Fellowship. One of the claims by converts to these movements is that they were attracted by the loving fellowship that was shown them, something they had not found in main-line churches where people seemed more concerned about themselves and going their own way. The religious community becomes their new family and its members their brothers and sisters. For many, such a group is even superior to their own natural families. There should be a warning here for main-line churches to cause a self-examination on the need for a greater sense of community.

Finally, we close with the thought with which we started this book. If you are going to discuss religion with the stranger at your door, know your own religion. This is of utmost importance. It is also advantageous to have some familiarity with the religion of the person to whom you speak, remembering that the same words do not always mean the same things; make certain that terms are defined before proceeding with the discussion at hand. If you see in the visitor at your door an opportunity, if you have love in your heart for that visitor, and if you have some of your visitor's zeal for souls, you can do much to lead that visitor to the fullness of Jesus Christ, who is the unknown God that person is really seeking.

Sources Consulted

General

Bjornstad, James. *Counterfeits at Your Door*. G/L Publications, 1979.

Burrell, Maurice C. *The Challenge of the Cults*. Baker Book House, 1984

Enroth, Ronald A. et al. *A Guide to Cults*. InterVarsity Press, 1983.

Passantino, Robert and Gretchen. *Answers to Cultists at Your Door*. Harvest House, 1981.

Whalen, William J. *Strange Gods*. Our Sunday Visitor, 1931.

_____. *Separated Brethren*. Our Sunday Visitor, 1979.

Jehovah's Witnesses

Awake! Watchtower Society. Various issues, 1987.

Hoekema, Anthony J. *Jehovah's Witnesses*. Eerdmans, 1986.

Morey, Robert J. *How to Answer a Jehovah's Witness*. Bethany House, 1980.

New World Translation of Holy Scriptures. Watchtower Society, 1961.

The Watchtower. Watchtower Society. Various issues, 1987.

Mormons

The Book of Mormon. Latter-Day Saints, 1963.

Fraser, Gordon H. *Is Mormonism Christian?* Moody Press, 1977.

Hoekema, Anthony J. *Mormonism.* Eerdmans, 1987.

Morey, Robert A. *How to Answer a Mormon.* Bethany House, 1983.

Pearl of Great Price. Latter-Day Saints, 1954.

Sackett, Chuck. *What's Going On In There?* Private printing, 1984.

Televangelists

Armstrong, Ben. *The Electric Church.* Thomas Nelson, 1979.

Hadden, Jeffery K. *Prime Time Preachers.* Addison Wesley, 1981.

Sholes, Jerry. *Give Me That Prime Time Religion.* Hawthorn Books, 1979.

Miscellaneous newspaper and magazine articles in personal file.

Index